W9-CBA-507

ABORTION

AND THE SANCTITY OF

Human Life

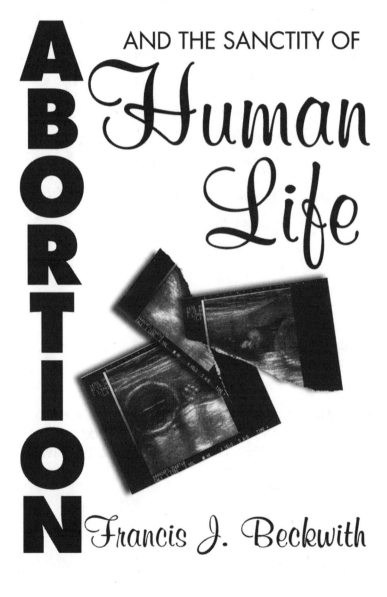

Francis J. Beckwith

 COLLEGE PRESS
PUBLISHING COMPANY
Joplin, Missouri

To my father and mother,
Harold "Pat" and
Elizabeth Beckwith.
For your 40th wedding anniversary
(January 23, 2000).
Thank you for being exemplars of not only life,
but the good life.

Copyright © 2000
College Press Publishing Co.
On the web at www.collegepress.com
Toll-free order line 1-800-289-3300

Cover design by Brett Lyerla

International Standard Book Number 0-89900-842-9

CONTENTS

745

112099

2000 AND BEYOND STUDIES FOR SMALL GROUPS

In pursuit of our stated goal, "Every Christian a Bible Student," College Press has, since 1995, been publishing a series of *Studies for Small Groups*. These have proved very popular, both for group and individual study on a variety of topics and Scripture texts. Although, with the year 2000, we have changed the outward appearance of these study booklets, our commitment is still to providing solid, thought-provoking studies that will make a life-changing difference in the reader.

Of course, although we call these studies "for small groups," they are equally suited for individual study. If you are simply reading the book for your own benefit, please do take the time to use the "Reflecting on . . ." questions to focus your own thoughts. In a small group study, the questions should not only be used as a review, to see if you remember what was actually said in that lesson by the writer, but to help spark discussion of the further *implications* of the lesson material. Nor should you consider the questions that are provided the only questions to be asked. Any study is only as good as the effort you put into it, and the group leader should have read the lesson through thoroughly before the class meets, as well as encouraging all other members of the group to do so if possible. If the leader has gone through the lesson in advance, he or she will probably have thought of other questions, some of which may never have even occurred to the writer or editors of the study. After all, what is important is not just the bare facts of the lesson, but how they intersect with your own path in the Christian walk.

Above all, do not feel you have to race through the lessons. Although the number of lessons is purposely kept small so that no one has to commit in advance to an endless period of time on the study, you should not cut off discussion of an important issue just to fit the whole of the lesson into one study session. Nor do you want to leave off the end of a lesson because you didn't get it all in during the allotted time. The greatest advantage of the small group setting is the flexibility you have, allowing you to carry over discussion to the next session. Take full advantage of this flexibility.

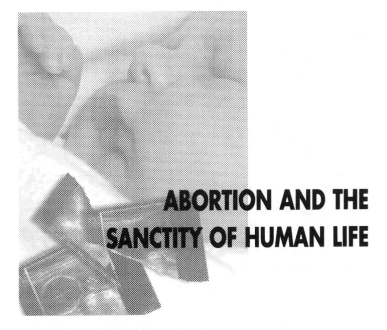

ABORTION AND THE SANCTITY OF HUMAN LIFE

The purpose of this small book is twofold: (1) to teach pro-life advocates how to better articulate and defend their viewpoint in the public square in an intelligent, gracious, and coherent manner, and (2) to provide an easy-to-read defense of the pro-life position for those who may be skeptical of its truth or curious about how it is defended.

Although this book is written so that it can be used for study in small groups, I think it will also be helpful to individuals who want to examine the issue in private reflection. Because this book is introductory and not a technical treatise in bioethics, jurisprudence, or political theory, readers should adjust their expectations accordingly. My hope, however, is to present a case against abortion rights and in support of unborn human beings that is accurate, fair, and does not compromise academic integrity, and yet is accessible to a wide range of people who, for differing reasons, would not ordinarily read technical literature on the subject.

A word about language. Unless quoting from another work, I will generally use the term "unborn" to describe the prenatal human being. The few times I do not use that term are when I am trying to accurately describe, in scientific and technical terms, the stages of prenatal human development. So, for example, the term *embryo* refers to the unborn between conception and the eighth week of pregnancy, while the term *fetus* refers to the unborn from the end of the eighth week until birth. However, the term *fetus* is typically used by some of the people and nonmedical works cited in this book to describe the unborn throughout all stages of pregnancy.

For those who are interested in more technical works that support the pro-life position, I recommend the following: Francis J. Beckwith, *Politically Correct Death: Answering the Arguments for Abortion Rights* (Baker, 1993); Patrick Lee, *Abortion & Unborn Human Life* (The Catholic University of America Press, 1996); and Stephen Schwarz, *The Moral Question of Abortion* (Loyola University Press, 1990). For a general introduction to bioethics, there are two outstanding works that one should consult: Scott B. Rae and Paul M. Cox, *Bioethics: A Christian Approach in a Pluralistic Age* (Eerdmans, 1999) and Mark W. Foreman, *Christianity and Bioethics: Confronting Clinical Issues* (College Press, 1999).

Although not a book on abortion per se, I highly recommend what is perhaps the most outstanding philosophical and theological defense of the pro-life view of the human person: J.P. Moreland and Scott B. Rae, *Body and Soul* (InterVarsity Press,

2000). For those who want to study the differing legal, philosophical, and political views on abortion, a place to start is the anthology *The Abortion Controversy 25 Years after* Roe v. Wade, 2nd ed., edited by Louis P. Pojman and Francis J. Beckwith (Wadsworth, 1998).

For those interested in practical training in defending the pro-life position, I highly recommend the publications of Scott Klusendorf. He can be reached at www.str.org.

ACKNOWLEDGMENTS

Special thanks to Tom Hess, editor of Focus on the Family's *Citizen Magazine*, for helping to edit and rework some portions of this text several years ago. Steve Cable and John Hunter of College Press deserve thanks for their dedication to publishing works that will benefit both the church and the wider culture.

I would also like to thank my good friend, Gregory Koukl, for his small though powerful booklet, *Precious Unborn Human Persons* (Stand to Reason, 1999). It is a testimony of what good writing, clear thinking, and philosophical sophistication can accomplish. It served as a model for what I am trying to achieve in this book.

With permission of Baker Book House, some portions of this small book are adapted from my larger work, *Politically Correct Death: Answering the Arguments for Abortion Rights* (Baker, 1993).

1

ABORTION AND THE NATURE
OF MORAL REASONING

In this lesson:

> ▶ Defining the issue
> ▶ Difference between preferences and moral claims
> ▶ Legal inconsistencies
> ▶ Living in the real world

---

*"The care of human life and happiness, and not their destruction,
is the first and only legitimate object of good government."*
—Thomas Jefferson

*"When Judge Douglas says that whoever, or whatever community,
wants slaves, they have a right to have them, he is perfectly logical*

Abortion and the Sanctity of Human Life

if there is nothing wrong in the institution; but if you admit that it is wrong, he cannot logically say that anybody has a right to do a wrong."
—Abraham Lincoln

"They got some beautiful people out there, man.
They can be a terror to your mind and show you how to hold your tongue
They got mystery written all over their foreheads
They kill babies in the crib and say only the good die young."
—Bob Dylan, from the song "Foot of Pride" (1983)

Why won't the abortion issue go away?

Most abortion advocates would like to end the debate. Now. And why shouldn't they expect to? They receive lavish media coverage, and spend millions on campaigns that appeal to the important notions of liberty, pluralism, and tolerance, but rarely if ever address the moral question of abortion.

So far, however, the return on their investment has been mush opinion polls and political and moral uncertainty. Take for example the following experience.

In February 1997 at a retreat for members of the Board of Trustees of a small liberal arts college in southern California, I spoke on the topic, "Can the Law Be Neutral on Moral Issues?" I lectured for about 45 minutes and then opened the floor for questions. One gentleman, an investment banker and attorney from New York City, said, "I agree with much of what you say Dr. Beckwith, but I think that on one issue, abortion, the law can remain neutral. You see, the current law, affirmed in the U.S. Supreme Court decisions *Roe v. Wade* and *Casey v. Planned Parenthood*, does not take a position on abortion. The law does not require women to have an abortion, and it does not forbid them from having an abortion. The law is neutral. The law is pro-choice." I replied to the gentleman that I did not agree with him but that the best way to understand my viewpoint would be to ask him questions in much the same way the ancient Greek philosopher Socrates questioned those with whom he dialogued. He thought the proposal was intriguing and agreed to participate. Our dialogue went something like this:

> "If fetuses were fully human, you would agree that abortions ought to be forbidden."

I asked, "Why do you think some people in our society oppose abortion?"

"Because they believe that fetuses are human beings or human persons."

"So you don't think they're right?"

"Yes."

"Then, what are fetuses?"

"They are potential persons or partial persons. They are not full human beings. So, I think killing them is wrong, but it's not like killing a full-fledged person. And that's why I think the government should stay out of the issue."

"But if fetuses were fully human, as pro-lifers assert, you would agree with them that virtually all abortions ought to be forbidden."

"Yes, that's right."

"So, your position is not really neutral, is it?"

"What do you mean?"

"You believe that if fetuses were fully human most abortions ought to be forbidden."

"That's correct."

"So, by allowing virtually unrestricted abortion, the govern-ment is taking a nonneutral position. It is saying that fetuses are not human persons, since, if they were, abortion would be unjustified homicide. Is this correct?"

"Yes. I now see your point. Pro-lifers believe that fetuses are fully human persons whereas pro-choicers do not. So, being pro-choice is not really neutral."

"That's right. The pro-choice perspective takes a position on who and what is a member of the human community, and con-cludes that the unborn are not included."

What my discussion with this gentleman reveals is something that is true of a large segment of the general public: they do not see abortion as a seri-ous wrong. Certainly, polling data have con-sistently shown that a vast majority of people see abortion as wrong, even morally wrong,

> In both practice and public discourse many people relegate abortion to a question of personal preference.

and they often describe it that way, using words and phrases like "tragic," "a difficult dilemma," "something I would never do," and "a horrible choice." But in both practice and public discourse they relegate abortion to a question of personal preference, something they do not do when it comes to behaviors they con-sider seriously wrong, such as spousal and child abuse, torture, and human slavery. For example, imagine the public's reaction to someone who said the following: "I am 'personally opposed' to owning a slave and torturing my spouse but if someone thought it consistent with his 'deeply held beliefs' to engage in such behaviors it would be wrong for me to try to force my beliefs on that person." A person having said that would be considered a moral monster. Yet, such language is perfectly acceptable when discussing abortion: "I am 'personally opposed' to abortion but if someone thought it consistent with her 'deeply held beliefs' to have an abortion it would be wrong for me to try to force my beliefs on that person." It is clear that even though a vast majority of Americans see abortion as morally wrong, many in that majority do not consider it a serious moral wrong.

Or perhaps they do not understand the nature of moral reasoning. That is, they believe that abortion is a serious moral wrong, on par with killing an adult human being without justification, but they do not understand what it means to say that something is morally wrong. If this is the case, it seems then that they are confusing moral claims with preference claims.

> Some people do not understand what it means to say that something is morally wrong.

THE NATURE OF MORAL REASONING

In order to understand this confusion, consider two statements:[1]

(1) I like vanilla ice cream

(2) Killing people without justification is wrong.

The first statement is a preference-claim, since it is a description of a person's subjective taste. It is not a *normative* claim. It is not a claim about what one ought or ought not to do. It is not saying, "Since I like vanilla ice cream, the government ought to coerce you to eat it as well" or "Everyone in the world ought to like vanilla ice cream too." A claim of subjective preference tells us nothing about what one *ought to* think or do. For example, if someone were to say, "I like to torture children for fun," this would tell us nothing about whether it is wrong or right to torture children for fun.

The second claim, however, is quite different. It has little if anything to do with what one likes or dislikes. In fact, one may *prefer* to kill another person without justification and still know that it is morally wrong to do so. This statement is a *moral claim*. It is not a descriptive claim, for it does not *describe* what, why, or how things are, or how a majority of people in fact behave and think. Nor is it a preference-claim, for it does not tell us what anyone's subjective preference may be or how one prefers to behave and think. Rather, it is a claim about what persons *ought to do*, which may be contrary to how persons in fact behave and how they prefer to behave.

People sometimes reduce a moral disagreement to a question of "personal preference" or "subjective opinion" rather than pondering and struggling with arguments for and against the position in question. Take for example the issue of whether parents and other concerned citizens have a right to boycott products that are advertised on television programs these citizens find to be morally inappropriate, especially for children. The usual reply to these citizens goes like this, "If you don't like a particular program, you don't have to

> One may actually *prefer* to do something which one knows is morally wrong.

watch it. You can always change the channel." But does the person who uses this reply really understand what these citizens are saying? After all, these citizens are not *merely* saying that they don't prefer these programs. In fact, these citizens and their children may actually be tempted to watch these programs; that is, in terms of sheer untutored appetite, they may actually *prefer* these programs, though they still *know* these programs are not *good* for them, just as one may prefer a candy bar but still know it's not good for her. To put it another way, these citizens are saying something a bit more subtle and profound than their detractors are likely to recognize, let alone admit: these programs convey messages and create a moral climate that will affect others, especially children, in a way that is adverse to the public good. Hence, what troubles these citizens is that *you* and *your children* may not change the channel. Furthermore, it bothers these people that there is probably somewhere in America an unsupervised ten-year-old who is, on a consistent basis, watching late night Home Box Office (HBO) or

> Some issues cannot be relegated to a question of one's personal preference.

listening to radio shock-jock Howard Stern or the latest gangsta rap CD. Most of these people fear that their ten-year-olds may have to socially interact with, and possibly date in the near future, this unsupervised ten-year-old. Others, who may not have young children, are concerned for the declining moral health of their communities, which sometimes is manifested in an increasing level of rudeness, disrespect, incivility, crime, or verbal and physical violence. Thus, this question cannot be relegated to a question of one's personal preference. The real question is whether there is any community or social action which is permissible and would best serve the public good.

Consider now the debate over abortion.[2] Many who defend a woman's right to abortion sometimes tell those who oppose abortion rights (pro-lifers): "Don't like abortion, then don't have one." This request reduces the abortion debate to a preference claim. That is, the moral rightness or wrongness of abortion — whether or not it involves killing an innocent human person — is declared, without argument, not relevant. But this is clearly a mistake, since those who oppose abortion do so because they believe that the fetus during most if not all of a woman's pregnancy is a human person with a right to life and it is generally wrong to violate a person's right to life. For this reason, when the pro-lifer hears the abortion advocate tell her that if she doesn't like abortion she doesn't have to have one, it sounds to her as if the abortion advocate is saying, "Don't like murder, then don't kill any innocent persons." Understandably, the pro-lifer finds such rhetoric perplexing as well as unpersuasive.

THE TENSION

Most arguments used to defend abortion, like the one presented by the gentleman I encountered at the college retreat, make sense only if they hold the same presupposition: that the unborn are not human persons and therefore do not require the community's protection. So, the most important question to answer in the abortion debate is this: Are the unborn human persons? I believe the correct answer to this question is "yes."

This truth is so fundamental that denying it leads even the best minds to the most absurd conclusions. Take, for example, the late Supreme Court Justice William O. Douglas. In the 1973 cases *Roe v. Wade* and *Doe v. Boston*, which legalized abortion for any time during pregnancy (see Lesson 2), Douglas agreed with the majority that unborn human beings were not persons under our Constitution and therefore had no right to life. Just the year before, however, in *Sierra Club v. Morton* (405 U.S. 727 [1972]) Douglas conferred legal rights on "valleys, alpine meadows,

rivers, lakes, estuaries, beaches, ridges, groves of trees, swamp-
land or even air that feels the destructive pressures of modern
technology and modern life. . . . the pileated woodpecker as well
as the coyote and bear, the lemmings as well as the trout in the
streams. . . . The voice of the inanimate object, therefore, should
not be stilled."[3]

In 1974, Charles Rice, then Dean of Notre Dame Law School,
commented that "the voice of the unborn child, according to
Justice Douglas, may be stilled any time his mother so desires.
So swamps and trees have rights, but the human child in the
womb has no rights."[4]

> Endangered species such as the California condor are protected even in embryo.

Other courts have
ruled that endan-
gered species — such
as the California con-
dor — are protected
in embryo. What is
the unborn child, if not a human individual deserving of a
greater chance to be born than endangered nonhuman species?

These inconsistencies are helpful in discussing abortion with
a family member, neighbor, or coworker. The late Christian
thinker, Francis Schaeffer, writes that when we communicate
with other people, we should understand that they live in tension between the "real world," as God created and ordered it,
and the logical conclusion of their presuppositions.

"When you face twentieth-century [or twenty-first century]
man, whether he is brilliant or an ordinary man of the street, a
man of the university or the docks, you are facing a man in tension; and it is this tension which works on your behalf as you
speak to him," Schaeffer writes. "A man may try to bury the tension and you may have to help him find it, but somewhere there

is a point of inconsistency. He stands in a position which he cannot pursue to the end."[5]

As we shall see, in the "real world" the unborn is unequivocally, uniquely a full-fledged member of the human community. When a person holds a presupposition that the unborn are not human persons, he is in conflict with the real world. Schaeffer writes: "There are no neutral facts, for facts are God's facts."[6]

Schaeffer argues that the best way to show a person how far he is from the real world, however, is to move him in the opposite direction — toward the logical conclusion of his presuppositions.

"We are pushing him towards the place where he ought to be, had he not stopped short," Schaeffer writes. "At that point of tension, he must analyze his beliefs, perhaps for the first time, and feel the pull of morals."[7]

NOTES

1. Hadley Arkes' work [*First Things: An Inquiry into the First Principles of Morality and Justice* (Princeton NJ: Princeton University Press, 1986)] was instrumental in helping me to articulate the difference between the two statements.

2. For an overview of the abortion debate from different sides, see Louis P. Pojman and Francis J. Beckwith, eds., *The Abortion Controversy 25 Years after* Roe v. Wade: *A Reader*, 2nd ed. (Belmont, CA: Wadsworth, 1998).

3. Cited in Michael E. Bauman, ed., *The Best of the Manion Forum* (San Francisco: Mellen Research University Press, 1990), p. 18.

4. Cited in Ibid.

5. Francis A. Schaeffer, *The God Who Is There* (Wheaton, IL: Crossway Books, 1968) as reprinted in *The Complete Works of Francis A. Schaeffer: A Christian Worldview*, vol. I (Wheaton, IL: Crossway Books, 1982), pp. 133-134.

6. Ibid., p. 138.

7. Ibid., pp. 138, 140.

19 Abortion and the Sanctity of Human Life

Reflecting on Lesson One

1. What is the most important question in the abortion debate and why?

2. Why do some abortion advocates believe that their view is "neutral," and why are they mistaken?

3. What is the difference between "preference claims" and "moral claims," and how does that difference help clarify the nature of the abortion debate?

4. Explain the inconsistency that seems to arise when one compares the U.S. Supreme Court's decision to permit abortion with Justice Douglas's affirmation of the rights of nonhuman living things?

5. Explain what Francis Schaeffer means by "the point of tension."

Consider this:

In preparation for lesson two, think about the exact nature of the unborn child. Read up on fetal development within the womb. Consider why some people are eager to see every slightest mark of growth in their unborn child's development, while others think of it as "womb contents."

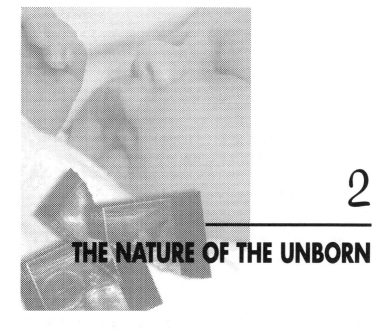

2

THE NATURE OF THE UNBORN

In this lesson:
▶ When does life begin, according to science?
▶ Stages of development within the womb
▶ Objections to seeing life as beginning at conception
— stated and answered

"We of today know that man is born of sexual union; that he starts life as an embryo within the body of the female; and that the embryo is formed from the fusion of two cells, the ovum and the sperm. . . . This seems so simple and evident to us that it is difficult to picture a time when it was not part of common knowledge."

—Dr. Alan F. Guttmacher, Planned Parenthood (1933)

Abortion and the Sanctity of Human Life

"Scientifically all we know is that a living human sperm unites with a living human egg; if they were not living there could be no union. . . . Does human life begin before or with the union of the gametes, or with birth, or at some intermediate time? I, for one, confess I do not know."

—Dr. Alan F. Guttmacher, Planned Parenthood (1973)

Because so much of the abortion debate revolves around the humanity of the unborn, as Dr. Guttmacher no doubt understood in both 1933 and 1973, it is crucial to review the facts of life. After all, many, like Dr. Guttmacher, who changed their minds about abortion when they saw the cultural and legal winds blowing in the direction of abortion rights, seem to confuse a change in mind with a change in facts. The former

What results from fertilization is a new biological entity.

does not entail the latter. So, for the sake of those who may read the 1973 version of Dr. Guttmacher and not the 1933 version, let's go over the facts.

THE FACTS OF LIFE [1]

As any biologist will tell you, life begins at conception — the point at which sperm and egg unite and cease to exist as individual entities. What results is a new entity, the zygote, a one-celled biological entity. It is a stage in human development through which each of us has passed (just as we have passed through infancy, childhood and adolescence). It is a misnomer to refer to this entity as a "fertilized ovum." For both ovum and sperm, which are genetically each a part of its owner (mother and father, respectively), cease to exist at the moment of conception. This new entity is clearly alive, for it meets all four criteria for life: metabolism, growth, reaction to stimuli, and reproduction.

The zygote is equipped with a unique genetic code, altogether different from the mother or father. From this point until death, no new genetic information is needed to make her a human individual. Her genetic make-up is established at conception, determining her physical characteristics — gender, eye color, bone structure, hair color, skin color, susceptibility to certain diseases, and more.

The only thing necessary for the growth and development of this human organism, as with the rest of us, is oxygen, shelter, food, and water.

> "The human nature of the human being from conception to old age is not a metaphysical contention, it is plain experimental evidence."

A subcommittee report of the U.S. Senate Judiciary Committee in 1981 cited both published medical texts and testimony from numerous scientific and bioethical authorities in conjunction with its study and analysis of the 1981 Human Life Bill. Here are excerpts from that report.

"To accept the fact that after fertilization has taken place a new human has come into being is no longer a matter of taste or opinion. The human nature of the human being from conception to old age is not a metaphysical contention, it is plain experimental evidence,"[2] testified French geneticist Jerome L. LeJeune.

Dr. Hyme Gordon, professor of medical genetics and a physician at the Mayo Clinic (Rochester, Minnesota), agreed with LeJeune:

[T]he question of the beginning of life—when life begins—is no longer a question of theological or philosophical dispute. It is an established scientific fact. Theologians and philosophers may go on to debate the meaning of life or the purpose of life, but it is an established fact that all life, including human life, begins at conception.

I have never ever seen in my own scientific reading, long before I became concerned with issues of life of this nature, that anyone has ever argued that life did not begin at the moment of conception and that it was a human conception that resulted from the fertilization of the human egg by a human sperm. As far as I know, these have never been argued against.[3]

Dr. Micheline Matthews-Roth, a research associate at Harvard Medical School, also testified: "[I]t is scientifically correct to say that an individual human life begins at conception, when egg and sperm join to form the zygote, and this developing human always is a member of our species in all stages of its life."[4]

"It is scientifically correct to say that an individual human life begins at conception."

Dr. M. Krieger writes in his book, *The Human Reproductive System*: "[A]ll organisms, however large, and complex they may be when fullgrown, begin life as but a single cell. This is true of the human being, for instance, who begins as a fertilized ovum."[5] Concurring with Dr. Krieger is Dr. B. Patten, who, in his text, *Human Embryology*, asserts: "The formation, maturation and meeting of a male and female sex cell are all preliminary to their actual union into a combined cell, or zygote, which definitely marks the beginning of a new individual."[6]

Here are a few familiar milestones in the development of pre-natal human life:[7]

✦ About three weeks after conception, a primitive heart begins to pulsate.

✦ In the first month, the liver, kidneys, digestive tract and umbilical cord begin to develop. The body has a head with primitive ears, mouth and eyes. The arms and legs begin to appear as tiny buds.

✦ Foundation for brain, spinal cord and central nervous system are established around the 21st day.

✦ During the second month, the child's skeleton develops, and her blood begins to flow. She has reflexes and her lips become sensitive to touch.

✦ At 33 days, the cerebral cortex, the part of the central nervous

At 40 to 43 days, brain waves can be detected.

system that governs motor activity as well as intellect, may be seen. At 40 to 43 days, brain waves can be detected.

✦ By the end of the seventh week, the baby bears the familiar external features and all the internal organs of the adult, even though it is less than an inch long and weighs only a tiny fraction of an ounce. It looks like a miniature baby.

✦ By the eighth week, her fingerprints start to form. Her stomach produces digestive juices, her liver manufactures blood cells and her kidneys extract uric acid from her blood stream.

After this point, according to a group of obstetricians, "everything is already present that will be found in the full-term baby. . . . From this point until adulthood, when full growth is achieved somewhere between 25 and 27 years, the changes in the body will mainly be in dimension and in gradual refinement of the working parts."[8]

terrible way to express this point!

Since the unborn can be brought into existence in a petri dish, as evidenced in the case of the so-called test-tube baby, and since this entity, if it has white parents, can be transferred to the womb of a black woman and be born white, we know conclusively that the unborn is not part of the woman's body.

So, from a strictly scientific point of view, there is no doubt that the development of an individual human life begins at conception. Consequently, it is vital that the reader understand that she did not come from a zygote, she once was a zygote; she did not come from an embryo, she once was an embryo; she did not come from a fetus, she once was a fetus; she did not come from an adolescent, she once was an adolescent. Consequently, each

> From a strictly scientific point of view, there is no doubt that the development of an individual human life begins at conception.

one of us has experienced these various developmental stages of life. None of these stages, however, imparted us with our humanity.

In light of this, it is interesting to note the conclusions of the U.S. Senate subcommittee mentioned above. It concluded that "no witness [who testified before the subcommittee] raised any evidence to refute the biological fact that from the moment of conception there exists a distinct individual being who is alive and is of the human species. No witness challenged the scientific consensus that unborn children are 'human beings,' insofar as the term is used to mean living beings of the human species." On the other hand, "those witnesses who testified that science cannot say whether unborn children are human beings were speaking in every instance to the value question rather than the scientific question. . . . [T]hese witnesses invoked their value preferences to redefine the term 'human being.'" The committee report explains that these witnesses "took the view that each person may define as 'human' only those beings whose lives that person wants to value. Because they did not wish to accord intrinsic worth to the lives of unborn children, they refused to call them 'human beings,' regardless of the scientific evidence."[9]

In Lesson 5 we will take a critical look at those who argue that even though the unborn is genetically a human being it is not a human *person*, and thus not entitled to the protection of the human community.

OBJECTIONS

In addition to the philosophical arguments we will cover in Lesson 5, some people put forth biological objections to individual human life beginning at conception. We will cover three of those objections here.

1. Sperm-Ovum Union Sometimes Does Not Result in a Human Being. According to one author, because "some entities that stem from the union of sperm and egg are not 'human beings' and never will develop into them," therefore, it is not correct to say that individual human life begins at conception.[10] The following are examples of such entities: the hydatidiform mole ("an entity which is usually just a degenerated placenta and typically has a random number of chromosomes"), the choriocarcinoma ("a 'conception-cancer' resulting from the sperm-egg union is one of gynecology's most malignant tumors"), and the blighted ovum ("a conception with the forty-six chromosomes but which is only a placenta, lacks an embryonic plate, and is always aborted naturally after implantation").[11]

The problem with this argument is that it misunderstands the pro-life case. The pro-lifer is *not* saying that everything that results from the union of sperm and ovum is the conception of an individual human being. Conception is one of *many results* of the union of sperm and ovum; it is *not* the *only* possible result. To put it another way: every ordinary conception of an individual human life is the result of a sperm-ovum union, but not every sperm-ovum union results in such a conception. Thus, the sperm-ovum union is a *necessary* condition for an ordinary conception, but *not* a sufficient condition.

2. The Cloning Objection: A Human Being May Come to Be apart from a Sperm-Ovum Union. Some people argue that since it is possible that some day there may be human beings, such as clones, who come into existence without the benefit of an ordinary sperm-egg union, therefore, it is not correct to say that individual human life begins at conception.[12] Prior to responding to this argument, it is important that we define cloning.

In early 1997, Dr. Ian Wilmut, a Scottish scientist, made headlines when he presented to the world, Dolly, a sheep he cloned from a six-year-old ewe. Three and one-half years earlier, Drs. Jerry Hall and Robert Stillman cloned a human embryo by successfully splitting one human embryo into two. Although this occurs naturally in the case of identical twins, Hall and Stillman were the first to replicate this process artificially.

Although many of us are acquainted with the concept of cloning because of popular films like *Multiplicity* and *The Boys from Brazil*, many of us do not know exactly what cloning is. When a scientist refers to "cloning," he may be speaking of one of two procedures: (A) embryo cloning; or (B) adult DNA cloning.

A. Embryo Cloning. This is the type of cloning performed by Hall and Stillman. It has been successfully used with animals for many years. Hall and Stillman began with what is called "in-vitro fertilization" or IVF: in a laboratory they produced in a petri dish human embryos by taking ova and fertilizing them with male sperm. Medical ethicist Scott B. Rae goes on to explain the process: "The embryos they used in their experiments had been fertilized by two sperm instead of one, making them abnormal embryos and destined to die within a week. This cloning process would be no different if the embryo were properly fertilized and had a normal chance at becoming a baby if implanted."[13] The reason why Hart and Stillman produced defective embryos rather than normal ones is that they did not intend for either the clones or the defective embryos to develop into babies.[14] They just wanted to see if they could artificially clone a human embryo.

In order to induce cloning, the following occurred. After the ovum was fertilized, the embryo divided in two, which is what occurs in normal development. The scientists then removed the zona pellucida,

Prior to considering when cloned life begins, it is important that we define cloning.

"the coating that contains enzymes that promote cell division that is necessary for growth and development." The two cells were then separated. Because development cannot continue unless the zona pellucida is replaced, Hall and Stillman "used an artificial zona pellucida to recoat the two embryonic cells, enabling development to continue. As the cells grow they form genetically identical embryos, a laboratory equivalent to what occurs naturally in the body when identical twins are conceived."[15] But because the embryos were defective, they perished after six days.[16]

Since this type of cloning is similar to the natural process of twinning (which will be covered below), our concern in this section will be adult DNA cloning.

B. Adult DNA Cloning. This is the type of cloning that produced Dolly the sheep. Because sheep, like human beings, are mammals, it is probable that in the future, perhaps the near future, scientists will be able to clone human beings by this method.

The DNA of every cell in the human body, except the sperm and ovum, contains the genetic material that in theory is capable of producing an identical clone of the body from which the cell is taken. But since the cells are programmed to perform certain functions (i.e., liver cells perform different functions than brain cells), and since all other functions are dormant, conception has to be replicated for a new and genetically identical human being to come into existence. This is accomplished by extracting the nucleus of a cell from a human body, fusing that cell with an ovum which has had its nucleus removed, and then electrically stimulating this fused entity. This is what occurred in the case of Dolly. But, according to molecular biologist Dr. Raymond Bohlin, "[t]he process was inefficient. Out of 277 cell fusions, 29 began growing in vitro. All 29 were implanted in receptive ewes, 13 became pregnant, and only one lamb was born as a result. This is a success rate of only 3.4%. In nature, somewhere between 33 and 50% of all fertilized eggs develop fully into newborns."[17]

> Whether human conception occurs as the result of sperm-ovum union or cloning is irrelevant.

If adult DNA cloning is performed on humans, a resulting clone will always be younger than her twin, unlike the adult clones of the character played by actor Michael Keaton in the film *Multiplicity*. So, if a 24-year-old woman clones herself, her cloned twin will always be 24 years her younger.

Why does adult DNA cloning not count against the pro-life view that individual life begins at conception? As with the first objection, the cloning argument confuses sperm-ovum union with conception. For if adult DNA cloning were to become a reality it would only mean that sperm-ovum conception is not a necessary condition for a human being to come into existence, just as sperm-ovum union is not a sufficient condition for an ordinary conception. To put it another way: whether human conception occurs as the result of sperm-ovum union or cloning is irrelevant; the entity that comes into existence is a human being and should be treated as such.

3. Twinning and Recombination Show that Individual Human Life Does Not Begin at Conception. Some people argue that since both twinning (the division of a conceived human) and recombination (the reuniting of the two) may occur up to fourteen days after conception, individual human life does not begin until division and recombination are no longer physically possible. There are several reasons we should reject this argument.

First, scientists are not agreed on many aspects of twinning. Some claim that twinning may be a nonsexual form of "parenting." This occurs in some animals and plants. Others claim that when twinning occurs an existing human being dies and gives life to two new and identical human beings like herself. Still others claim that since not all human embryos have the natural capacity to twin, one could argue that there exists in some embryos a basic duality prior to the split. Hence, it is claimed that at least in some incipient form two individual lives were present from the start of conception. In any event, the fact of twinning does not seem to be a sufficient reason to abandon the belief that individual human life begins at conception.[18]

Second, every conceived human, whether before twinning or recombination, is still a human individual who is genetically distinct from her parents. In other words, simply because identical twins result from the splitting of a conceived human or one individual results from two that recombine, it does not follow that any of the human entities prior to twinning or recombining were not individual human beings.[19] To help us understand this point, Robert Wennberg provides the following story:

> Imagine that we lived in a world in which a certain percentage of teenagers replicated themselves by some mysterious natural means, splitting in two upon reaching their sixteenth birthday. We would not in the least be inclined to conclude that no human being could therefore be considered a person prior to becoming sixteen years of age; nor would we conclude that life could be taken with greater impunity prior to replication than afterward. The real oddity — to press the parallel — would be two teenagers becoming one. However, in all of this we still would not judge the individual's claim to life to be undermined in any way. We might puzzle over questions of personal identity . . . but we would not allow these strange replications and fusions to influence our thinking about an individual's right to life. Nor therefore does it seem that such considerations are relevant in determining the point at which an individual might assume a right to life in utero.[20]

These objections concern questions of individual human life during the first moments and/or days of human existence, not when most women discover they are pregnant.

It should be noted that even if these three objections were

correct, this would not help the defender of abortion rights, for these objections concern questions of individual human life during the first moments and/or days of human existence. Since the unborn is well on its way in human development when a vast majority of women discover they are pregnant, these objections are not practically relevant in virtually every case of pregnancy.

CONCLUSION

The pro-life advocate believes that individual human life begins at conception for at least four reasons: (1) At the moment of conception a separate human individual with its own genetic code and needing only food, water, shelter, and oxygen in order to grow and develop, comes into existence. (2) Like the infant, the child, the adolescent, the unborn is a being who is in the process of becoming. She is not a becoming who is striving toward being. She is not a potential human life but a human life with great potential. (3) The unborn is the sexual product of human parents, and a developing unborn entity that is the sexual product of members of a

> The same being that begins as a zygote continues to birth and adulthood with no decisive break.

particular mammalian species is itself an individual member of that species. (4) The same being that begins as a zygote continues to birth and adulthood. There is no decisive break in the continuous development of the human entity from conception until natural death that would make this entity a different being before birth. This is why it makes perfect sense to say, "When I was conceived. . . ." It is, therefore, apparent from the biological facts that although the unborn develops from a less complex to a more complex creature, it does not change from one being into another being. It is human from the start.

NOTES

1. These facts of human development in this section draw from numerous texts and essays, including the following: F. Beck, D.B. Moffat, and D.P. Davies, *Human Embryology*, 2nd ed. (Oxford: Blackwell, 1985); Keith L. Moore, *The Developing Human: Clinically Oriented Embryology*, 2nd ed. (Philadelphia: W.B. Saunders, 1977); Andre E. Hellegers, "Fetal Development," in *Biomedical Ethics*, eds. Thomas A. Mappes and Jane S. Zembatty (New York: Macmillan, 1981); Stephen M. Krason, *Abortion: Politics, Morality, and the Constitution* (Lanham, MD: University Press of America, 1984); Bart T. Hefferman, "The Early Biography of Everyman," in *Abortion and Social Justice*, eds. Thomas W. Hilgers, MD, and Dennis J. Horan, Esq. (New York: Sheed & Ward, 1972), pp. 3-25; *Motion and Brief Amicus Curiae of Certain Physicians, Professors, and Fellows of the American College of Obstetrics and Gynecology in Support of Appellees*, submitted to the Supreme Court of the United States, October Term, 1971, No. 70-18, *Roe v. Wade*, and No. 70-40, *Doe v. Bolton*, prepared by Dennis J. Horan, et al. (The list of amici contains the names of more than two hundred physicians), as quoted in Stephen D. Schwarz, *The Moral Question of Abortion* (Chicago: Loyola University Press, 1990), pp. 2-6.

2. *The Human Life Bill: Hearings on S. 158 before the Subcommittee on Separation of Powers of the Senate Judiciary Committee*, 97th Congress, 1st Session (1981), as quoted in Norman L. Geisler, *Christian Ethics: Options and Issues* (Grand Rapids: Baker, 1989), p. 149.

3. *The Human Life Bill—S. 158, Report together with Additional and Minority Views to the Committee on the Judiciary, United States Senate, made by its Subcommittee on Separation of Powers*, 97th Congress, 1st Session (1981): 9.

4. Ibid., p. 8.

5. Ibid., pp. 7, 8. This quote is taken from Dr. Krieger's book, *The Human Reproductive System* (1969), p. 88.

6. *The Human Life Bill—Report*, p. 8. The quote is taken from Dr. Patten's book, *Human Embryology*, 3rd ed. (1968): p. 43.

7. See the works cited in note 1.

8. *Motion and Brief Amicus Curiae of Certain Physicians, Professors, and Fellows of the American College of Obstetrics and Gynecology in Support of Appelees*, pp. 3,4.

9. *The Human Life Bill—Report*, p. 11.

10. Bernard Nathanson (with Richard Ostling), *Aborting America* (New York: Doubleday, 1979), p. 214.

11. Ibid.

12. For a summary of the philosophical and scientific problems surrounding human cloning, see Andrew Varga, *The Main Issues in Bioethics*, 2nd ed. (New York: Paulist, 1984), pp. 119-126.

13. Scott B. Rae, *Brave New Families: Biblical Ethics and Reproductive Technologies* (Grand Rapids: Baker, 1996), pp. 172-173.

14. Connie Cass, "Spotlight thrust on scientists who cloned human embryos," *Las Vegas Review-Journal* (October 23, 1993): 1A, 2A.

15. Rae, *Brave New Families*, p. 173.

16. Rae's description of the technical procedure is taken from Philip Elmer-Dewitt, "Cloning: Where Do We Draw the Line?" *Time* (November 8, 1993): 67.

17. Raymond G. Bohlin, "The Little Lamb that Made a Monkey of Us All," (March 7, 1997), available online at: www.probe.org/docs/lambclon.html.

18. See Varga, *Main Issues in Bioethics*, pp. 64-65.

19. See Ibid., p. 65.

20. Robert Wennberg, *Life in the Balance: Exploring the Abortion Controversy* (Grand Rapids: Eerdmans, 1985), p. 71.

Reflecting on Lesson Two

1. Why is it reasonable to believe that the unborn is a human being from the moment of conception? What are some of the biological facts of human development that one can use in defending this perspective?

2. What are the two different types of cloning?

3. Why do some people believe that cloning counts against human life beginning at conception? How would you respond to this argument?

4. Why do some people believe that twinning and recombination count against human life beginning at conception? How would you respond to this argument?

5. Some people deny that life begins at conception based on the fact that the sperm-ovum union sometimes does not result in a human being. How do they defend this argument and how would you respond to it?

Consider this:

What do you know about the legal status of abortion? What does U.S. and state law now permit and what does the law prohibit? Do you know? To prepare for lesson three, see what you can find out. Consider the difference between actual fact and public perception on this subject.

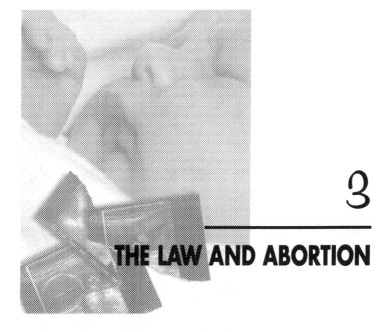

3

THE LAW AND ABORTION

In this lesson:

▶ The background of *Roe v. Wade*
▶ The relevance of Lesson Two to the legal arguments
▶ Modifications to abortion law by the *Webster* and *Casey* decisions

---

"Anyone in America who writes these days about abortion must take account of the landmark decision of the Supreme Court in Roe v. Wade; and in estimating the 'quality of mind' manifested by the Court, he would have to regard that profundity which stands near the beginning of Justice Blackmun's opinion for the majority: 'Pregnancy often comes more than once to the same woman, and . . . if man is to survive, [pregnancy] will always be with us.' One becomes aware instantly that one is in the presence of no ordinary mind."

—Professor Hadley Arkes, *First Things* (1986)

Abortion and the Sanctity of Human Life

The legal nature of the abortion debate is often misunderstood. There is a widespread misperception that the U.S. Supreme Court's most important decision on abortion, *Roe v. Wade* (1973), is moderate and does not allow for abortion on demand, the right to virtually unrestricted abortion for all nine months of pregnancy. For this reason, it is necessary that we study and understand the U.S. Supreme Court's major decisions on abortion.

ROE v. WADE AND THE BEGINNING OF HUMAN LIFE

The case of *Roe v. Wade* (1973) concerned Jane Roe (a.k.a. Norma McCorvey), a resident of Texas, who claimed to have become pregnant as a result of a gang rape (which was found later to be a false charge). According to the Texas law at the time (essentially unchanged since 1856), a woman can have an abortion only if it is necessary in order to save her life. Because Roe's pregnancy was not life-threatening, she sued the state of Texas. In 1970, the unmarried Roe filed a class action suit in federal court in Dallas. The federal court ruled that the Texas law was unconstitutionally vague and overbroad and infringed on a woman's right to reproductive freedom. The state of Texas appealed to the U.S. Supreme Court. After the case was argued twice before the Court, on January 22, 1973, the Court in *Roe v. Wade* agreed with the federal district court and ruled that the Texas law

> The Supreme Court ruled that all states must permit abortions not only in cases of rape but also in all cases.

was unconstitutional and that not only must all states including Texas permit abortions in cases of rape but also in all cases.

In *Roe*, the Court divided pregnancy into trimesters. It ruled that aside from normal procedural guidelines to insure protection for the pregnant woman, a state has no right to restrict abortion in the first six months of pregnancy. Thus a woman could have an abortion in the first six months of pregnancy for any reason. In the last trimester (after the unborn is viable) the state has a right, although no obligation, to restrict abortions to only those cases in which the mother's life or health is in danger, since the state may have a legitimate interest in prenatal life. But the Court's "health restriction" is a restriction in name only, for in *Roe*'s companion decision *Doe v. Bolton* (1973), the Court ruled that "health" must be taken in its broadest possible context, defined "in light of all factors — physical, emotional, psychological, familial, and the woman's age — relevant to the well-being of the patient. All these factors relate to health."[1] This is why a U.S. Senate subcommittee concluded in 1981 that "since there is nothing to stop an abortionist

> In *Doe v. Bolton*, the Court ruled that the "health" of the mother must be taken in its broadest possible context.

from certifying a third-trimester abortion is beneficial to the health of the mother — in this broad sense — the Supreme Court's decision has in fact made abortion available on demand throughout the pre-natal life of the child, from conception to birth."[2]

What about the evidence of fetal humanity that we covered earlier in Lesson 2? Did the Court take that into consideration? Not really. Although Justice Harry Blackmun, in his majority opinion, mentions different views about when life begins, he claims that the Court should not take a side on the question: "We need not resolve the difficult question of when life begins. When those trained in the respective disciplines of medicine, philosophy, and theology are unable to arrive at any consensus, the judiciary, at this point in the development of man's knowledge, is not in a position to speculate"[3]

Justice Blackmun is arguing that because experts disagree as to when life begins, the Court should not come down on any side. Hence, the government should not take one theory of life and force those who do not agree with that theory to subscribe to it, which is the reason why Blackmun writes in *Roe*, "In view of all this, we do not agree that, by adopting one theory of life, Texas may override the rights of the pregnant woman that are at stake."[4] That is, because experts disagree about when and if the fetus becomes a human life, then abortion should remain legal.

In popular debate Justice Blackmun's claim is often put forth by abortion advocates when they affirm that "no one knows when life begins," and from that affirmation conclude that abortion ought to be legally permitted. There is a difference, however, between claiming that "no one knows when life begins" and "experts disagree as to when life begins." My guess is that when people use the former in popular debate, they are in fact arguing that it is justified by the latter:

(1) Experts disagree as to when life begins

Therefore,

(2) No one knows when life begins

Of course (2) does not necessarily follow from (1). It may be that experts disagree as to when human life begins but some of them are wrong while others in fact know when human life begins. This would not be surprising, since historically some faction of experts usually turns out to be correct about a disputed issue, such as in the cases of slavery, women's suffrage, and the position of the Earth in the solar system. In some cases expert disagreement can be accounted for by some factions ignoring contrary evidence or alternative theories, for reasons having to do with a prior commitment to a worldview. In other cases expert disagreement may result from holding an irrational belief, clinging to a religious or secular dogma, or not wanting to appear politically incorrect. By treating all expert disagreement over the nature of unborn life as philosophically and scientifically indistinguishable, by giving the impression that all the arguments of all the factions in the debate are equally com-

> Expert disagreement may result from holding an irrational belief.

pelling, and by simply appealing to expert disagreement rather than wrestling with the actual arguments put forth by these experts and evaluating these arguments for their logical soundness, the Court was able to simply discard the issue of the unborn's humanity while pretending to actually take it into consideration.

The claim, however, that "no one knows when life begins" is a misnomer, since, as we have seen (Lesson 2), virtually no one seriously doubts that individual biological human life is present from conception.[5] Thus, what Blackmun and other abortion advocates probably mean when they say that "no one knows when life begins" is that no one knows when personhood or *full* humanness is attained in the process of human development by the individual in the womb. That is to say, no one knows when the unborn becomes a full member of the human community and worthy of protection.[6] In Lesson 5 we will critique this notion that there could be human beings that are not persons.

But is Justice Blackmun correct in saying that the Court "is not in a position to speculate" and for that reason has taken an apparently neutral stance on the unborn's humanity and is not "adopting one theory of life" over another? Far from it. Consider the following three points.

First, to claim, as Justice Blackmun does, that the Court should not propose one theory of life over another, and that the decision to abort should be left exclusively to the discretion of each pregnant woman, is to propose a theory of life which hardly has a clear consensus. For it has all the earmarks of a theory of life that morally segregates the unborn from full-fledged membership in the human community, for it in practice excludes the unborn from constitutional protection. Although verbally the Court denied taking sides, its legal opinion is in fact saying that the unborn in this society is not a being worthy of protection.

Although verbally the Court denied taking sides, its legal opinion is in fact saying that the unborn in this society is not a being worthy of protection.

Thus, the Court actually did take sides on when life begins. It concluded that the fetus is not a human person, since the procedure permitted in *Roe*, abortion, is something that the Court itself admits it would not have ruled a fundamental right if it were conclusively proven that the fetus is a human person: "The appellee and certain amici argue that the fetus is a 'person' within the language and meaning of the Fourteenth Amendment. In support of this, they outline at length and in detail the well-known facts of fetal development. *If this suggestion of personhood is established,* the appellant's case, of course, collapses, for the fetus' right to life would then be guaranteed specifically by the Amendment"[7] [emphasis added].

Imagine if the Court were confronted with the issue of enslaving African-Americans and delivered the following opinion: "We need not resolve the difficult question of whether blacks are human persons. When those trained in the respective disciplines of medicine, philosophy, and theology are unable to arrive at any consensus, the judiciary, at this point in the development of man's knowledge, is not in a position to speculate." Suppose that the Court on that basis *allowed* white Americans to own blacks as property, concluding that slave ownership is a fundamental right. It would appear that although the Court would be making a verbal denial of taking any position on this issue, the allowance of slavery and the claim that it is a fundamental right would for all intents and purposes be morally equivalent to taking a side on the issue, namely, that blacks are not human persons. Likewise, the Court's verbal denial of taking a position on the unborn's personhood is contradicted by its conclusion that abortion is a fundamental constitutional right and that the unborn are not persons under the Constitution.

Second, if we are to accept the Supreme Court's holding in *Roe*, and agree with Justice Blackmun that the right to abortion is contingent upon the status of the unborn, then the allegedly disputed fact about life's

> The allegedly disputed fact about life's beginning means that the right to abortion is disputed as well.

beginning means that the right to abortion is disputed as well. For a conclusion's support — in this case, "abortion is a fundamental right" — is only as good as the truth of its most important premise — in this case, "the unborn is not a human person." So, the Court's admission that abortion-rights is based on a widely disputed fact, far from establishing a right to abortion, entails that the Court, not only does not know when life begins, but it does not know when if ever the right to abortion begins.

Third, if it is true that no one knows when life begins, this is an excellent reason not to permit abortion, since an abortion may result in the death of a human person who has a full right to life. If one killed another being without knowing whether the being is a person with a full right to life, such an action would be negligent, even if one later discovered that the being was not a person. If game hunters shot at rustling bushes with the Court's mind-set, the National Rifle Association's membership would become severely depleted. Ignorance of a being's status is certainly not justification to kill it.

> Ignorance of a being's status is certainly not justification to kill it.

WEBSTER AND CASEY

In *Webster v. Reproductive Health Services* (1989),[8] the Court reversed a lower-court decision and upheld a Missouri statute that contains several provisions, one of which forbids physicians to perform abortions after the fetus is twenty weeks old, except when the woman's life is in imminent danger. The statute requires a physician, if he believes that his pregnant patient seeking an abortion may be twenty weeks pregnant, to have her undergo a test in order to determine the unborn's gestational age. *Webster* modified *Roe* in at least two significant ways. First, it rejected *Roe's* trimester breakdown of pregnancy. Chief Justice William Rehnquist, who wrote the majority opinion in the 5 to 4 decision, argued that the trimester breakdown is not found in the Constitution and that the Court sees no reason why a state's interest in protecting the unborn should arrive at the point of viability. Second, the Court in *Webster* ruled as constitutional the portion of the Missouri statute that forbade the use of government funds and employees in performing and counseling for a nontherapeutic abortion. Although chipping away at the foundation of *Roe*, *Webster* did not overturn it.

In *Planned Parenthood v. Casey* (1992) the Court was asked to consider the constitutionality of five provisions of the Pennsylvania Abortion Control Act of 1982. The Court upheld as constitutional four of the five provisions, rejecting the third one (which required spousal notification) based on what it calls the *undue burden* standard. This is a departure from *Roe*, for *Roe* affirms abortion as a fundamental constitutional right and thus makes any possible restrictions subject to strict scrutiny. In other words, possible restrictions, in order to be valid, must be essential to meeting a compelling public need. For example, laws that forbid yelling "fire" in a crowded theater pass strict scrutiny and thus do not violate the First Amendment right to freedom of expression. But the *Casey* court, by subscribing to the undue burden standard, does not support the right to abortion as fundamental. Therefore, the states may restrict abortion by passing laws that

> By subscribing to the undue burden standard, the *Casey* court does not support the right to abortion as fundamental.

may not withstand strict scrutiny but nevertheless do not result in an undue burden for the pregnant woman. Admitting that the undue burden standard "has no basis in constitutional law," the Court suggests that when lower courts apply this standard when evaluating abortion regulations, "judges will have to make the subjective, unguided determination whether the regulations place 'substantial obstacles' in the path of a woman seeking an abortion, undoubtedly engendering a variety of conflicting views."[9]

The *Casey* court upheld *Roe* as a precedent, despite the fact that it rejected three important aspects of *Roe*: (1) its trimester framework (which *Webster* rejected as well); (2) that a woman has a fundamental right to abortion; and (3) its requirement that restrictions be subject to strict scrutiny. Perhaps this is why Chief Justice Rehnquist made the comment in his dissenting opinion in *Casey*: "*Roe* continues to exist, but only in the way a storefront on a western movie set exists: a mere facade to give the illusion of reality."[10]

There is one passage from Casey which has received attention in the literature, because it seems to constitutionally ground the right to abortion in "the right to personal autonomy," something that did not seem explicitly to be part of the Court's decision in *Roe*. The passage reads:

> "*Roe* continues to exist, but only in the way a storefront on a western movie set exists: a mere facade to give the illusion of reality."

> Our law affords constitutional protection to personal decisions relating to marriage, procreation, family relationships, child rearing, and education. . . . These matters, involving the most intimate and personal choices a person may make in a lifetime, choices central to personal dignity and autonomy, are central to the liberty protected by the Fourteenth Amendment. At the heart of liberty is the right to define one's own concept of existence, of meaning, of the universe, and of the mystery of human life. Beliefs about these matters could not define the attributes of personhood were they formed under compulsion by the State.[11]

It is no wonder that some commentators have called this the "mystery passage,"[12] though lower courts have found it to be no mystery at all, and have interpreted the passage to mean that personal autonomy trumps nearly every state interest in one's personal decision making. For example, in a 1994 U.S. District Court case in which the court ruled that a prohibition against physician-assisted suicide is unconstitutional, *Compassion in Dying v. Washington*, Judge Barbara Rothstein employed the logic of Casey:

> Like the abortion decision, the decision of a terminally ill person to end his or her life "involves the most intimate and personal choices a person can make in a lifetime," and constitutes a "choice central to personal dignity and autonomy."[13]

The U.S. Supreme Court seems for the time being to have rejected this interpretation of *Casey* when on June 26, 1997, it overturned both Judge Rothstein's ruling as well as an opinion delivered by a federal appeals court that upheld her ruling.[14] Nevertheless, it is an interpretation which finds acceptance among some of the more influential social and legal philosophers. For instance, consider the comments of Ronald Dworkin, perhaps the most influential contemporary legal philosopher:

> Our Constitution takes no sides in these ancient disputes about life's meaning. But it does protect people's right to die as well as live, so far as possible, in the light of their own intensely personal convictions about "the mystery of human life." It insists that these values are too central to personality, too much at the core of liberty, to allow a majority to decide what everyone must believe.[15]

CONCLUSION

The Supreme Court currently affirms a woman's right to abortion during the entire nine months of pregnancy, allowing states only to make restrictions that do not entail an undue burden.

Thus, according to the current legal regime in the United States, the unborn, despite the overwhelming evidence of its humanity and its existence, is not protected by the U.S. Constitution.

NOTES

1. *Doe v. Bolton* 410 U.S. 179, 192 (1973).

2. *The Human Life Bill—S. p. 158, Report together with Additional and Minority Views to the Committee on the Judiciary, United States Senate, made by its Subcommittee on Separation of Powers,* 97th Congress, 1st Session (1981): 5. Among the scores of works which address this legal issue are the following: John Hart Ely, "The Wages of Crying Wolf: A Comment on *Roe v. Wade,*" *Yale Law Journal* 82 (1973): 921; Lynn Wardle and Mary Anne Q. Wood, *A Lawyer Looks at Abortion* (Provo, UT: Brigham Young University Press, 1982), p. 12; Stephen M. Krason, *Abortion: Politics, Morality, and the Constitution* (Lanham, MD: University Press of America, 1984), pp. 103-104; Francis J. Beckwith, *Politically Correct Death: Answering the Arguments for Abortion Rights* (Grand Rapids: Baker, 1993), chapter 2; Jacqueline Nolan Haley, "Haunting Shadows from the Rubble of *Roe's* Right to Privacy," *Suffolk University Law Review* 9 (1974): 152-153; Roger Wertheimer, "Understanding Blackmun's Argument: The Reasoning of *Roe v. Wade,*" in *Abortion: Moral and Legal Perspectives,* eds. Jay L. Garfield and Patricia Hennessy (Amherst, MA: University of Massachusetts Press, 1984), 120-121; and Mary Anne Glendon, *Abortion and Divorce in Western Law* (Cambridge, MA: Harvard University Press, 1987), pp. 22-24.

3. *Roe v. Wade* 410 U.S. 113, 160 (1973).

4. Ibid., p. 163.

5. This has been challenged by C.A. Bedate and R.C. Cefalo in their essay, "The Zygote: To Be or Not to Be a Person," *Journal of Medicine and Philosophy* 14 (1989). Their case, however, is seriously flawed. See the following replies: Patrick Lee, *Abortion and Unborn Human Life* (Washington, DC: The Catholic University of America Press, 1996), pp. 98-102; and Antoine Suarez, "Hydatidiform Moles and Teratomas Confirm the Human Identity of the Preimplantation Embryo," *Journal of Medicine and Philosophy* 15 (1990).

6. It should be noted, as we shall see in Lesson 5, that there are some scholars who argue that they *do know* when human life becomes morally valuable. They maintain that at some decisive moment during pregnancy or

after birth the unborn (or newborn) acquires certain properties that make him a human person (or moral human being) rather than merely a human being (or genetically human). For defenses of a variety of views on when after conception this decisive moment occurs, see the essays by Michael Tooley, Louis Pojman, L.W. Sumner, Gerald H. Paske, and Jane English in Louis Pojman and Francis J. Beckwith, eds., *The Abortion Controversy 25 Years after* Roe v. Wade: *A Reader*, 2nd ed. (Belmont, CA: Wadsworth, 1998). For critiques of these and other views, see Beckwith, *Politically Correct Death*; Baruch Brody, *Abortion and the Sanctity of Human Life: A Philosophical View* (Cambridge, MA: MIT Press, 1975); Lee, *Abortion and Unborn Human Life*; J.P. Moreland and Scott B. Rae, *Body and Soul* (Downers Grove, IL: InterVarsity Press, 2000); Stephen Schwarz, *The Moral Question of Abortion* (Chicago: Loyola University Press, 1990); and Don Marquis, "Why Abortion Is Immoral," *The Journal of Philosophy* 86 (April 1989).

7. *Roe v. Wade*, 157-158.

8. *Webster v. Reproductive Health Services* U.S. 490 (1989).

9. *Planned Parenthood v. Casey* U.S., nos. 91-744 and 91-902 (1992): I (Syllabus).

10. Ibid., p. 12 (Rehnquist J., dissenting).

11. *Planned Parenthood v. Casey*, 112 Sup. Ct. 2791, 2807 (1992) Although this is the same decision cited in the previous two notes, this present citation comes from a different text of Casey.

12. See Gerard V. Bradley, "Shall We Ratify the New Constitution?: The Judicial Manifesto in *Casey* and *Lee*," in *Benchmarks: Great Constitutional Controversies in the Supreme Court*, ed. Terry Eastland (Washington, DC: Ethics and Public Policy Center/Grand Rapids: Eerdmans, 1995), pp. 117-140.

13. As quoted in Timothy Egan, "Federal Judge Says Ban on Suicide Aid Is Unconstitutional," *The New York Times* (5 May 1994): A24.

14. *Washington v. Glucksberg* U.S., no. 96-110 (1997); and *Vacco v. Quill* U.S., no. 95-1858 (1997).

15. Ronald Dworkin, "When Is It Right to Die?," *The New York Times* (17 May 1994): A19.

Reflecting on Lesson Three

1. What did the Supreme Court in *Roe v. Wade* rule concerning the legality of abortion?

2. Did the Supreme Court in *Roe v. Wade* conclude anything about the nature of the unborn? Give at least three reasons why its conclusion is inadequate.

3. How did the *Webster* decision change abortion law?

4. How did the *Casey* decision change abortion law?

Consider this:

What arguments have you heard people use in favor of abortion? Before going into lesson four, think about how you would answer those arguments. Then see how the writer's answers compare with yours.

$$4$$

POPULAR ARGUMENTS
FOR ABORTION RIGHTS

In this lesson:

▶ Arguments from illegal abortions, unwanted children, etc.

▶ Attacks made on pro-life advocates

▶ Issues of the viability of the child and the life of the mother

*The most merciful thing a large family can do
for one of its infant members is to kill it.*

—Margaret Sanger, founder of Planned Parenthood (1920)

*We have to remind people that abortion is the guarantor of a woman's right
to participate in the social and political life of society.*

—Kate Michelman, abortion rights advocate (1988)

Whenever people receive their first serious instruction on the abortion issue, it comes as a shock to many of them that virtually all the popular arguments for abortion fail. That does not mean, of course, that the general public as well as some of our most celebrated talking heads do not find these bad arguments persuasive. Rather, it means that many people, if not most people, do not understand the nature of moral reasoning and how to apply it consistently to an issue as serious as abortion. In order to remedy this lack, in this lesson we will evaluate bad arguments for abortion rights. Even though this list is by no means exhaustive, our analysis of these arguments can be applied to most other popular abortion rights arguments that we could not cover in this lesson.[1]

ARGUMENT FROM ILLEGAL ABORTIONS

Some argue that if abortion is made illegal, then women will once again be harmed by unsafe and illegal abortions performed by back-alley butchers, as they were before *Roe v. Wade*. Therefore, abortion ought to remain legal. This argument, though evoking sympathy with the public, is seriously flawed.

First, it *assumes* that the unborn is not a human person. But only by making this controversial assumption does the argument work. For if the unborn is a human person, this argument is tantamount to saying that because people die or are harmed while killing other people (the unborn), the government should make it safe for them to do so. Even Mary Anne Warren, an abortion rights

> Because people die or are harmed while killing other people, should the government make it safe for them to do it?

supporter, clearly sees the inadequacy of this argument: "[T]he fact that restricting access to abortion has tragic side effects does not, in itself, show that the restrictions are unjustified, since murder is wrong regardless of the consequences of prohibiting it."[2] Thus, one must *first answer* the question of whether the unborn are human persons *before* one can say with any confidence whether abortion ought or ought not to be permitted.

Second, this argument assumes that the illegal abortions prior to *Roe* were performed almost exclusively by incompetent nonphysicians. Yet former president of Planned Parenthood, Dr. Mary Calderone, wrote in 1960 that "90% of all illegal abortions are done by physicians. . . . Whatever trouble arises usually comes after self-induced abortions which comprise approximately eight percent, or with the very small percentage that go to some kind of nonmedical abortionist. Another corollary fact: Physicians of impeccable standing are referring their patients for these illegal abortions to the colleagues they know are willing to perform them."[3]

> This argument assumes that the illegal abortions were performed almost exclusively by incompetent nonphysicians.

Abortion rights supporters also claim that "thousands of women" died from illegal abortions every year prior to *Roe.*[4] But if that's true, then they died at the hands of licensed physicians in "good standing" who later became the practitioners of "safe, legal" abortion.

Nearly 20 years after Calderone's article was published, Faye Wattleton, then-president of Planned Parenthood, made a claim that seems to contradict Calderone's numbers. Ignoring Calderone's claim that 90% of all illegal abortions were performed by licensed physicians, Wattleton claimed in 1979 that only five percent of illegal abortions in the 1960s were performed by licensed practitioners.[5] What accounts for the switch from 90% to five percent? Wattleton provided no answer.

Nevertheless, at the end of the day, the number of illegal abortions and who performed them prior to *Roe* are morally and constitutionally irrelevant. After all, if the unborn are not human persons, then abortion need not be justified by appealing to anything, let alone illegal and dangerous abortions. On the other hand, if the unborn are human persons, then it makes no sense to claim that the government ought to make it safer to kill such persons because people participating in the killing may be harmed.

> Arguments for abortion work only if one *assumes* that the unborn are not human persons.

ARGUMENT FROM PREVENTING CHILD ABUSE

Many in the abortion rights movement argue that legal abortion will help to eliminate unwanted children. They further argue that "unwantedness" is indirectly responsible for a great number of family problems such as child abuse. Therefore, abortion is needed in order to stem the tide of child abuse. This argument is flawed for many reasons.

First, like so many others used to support abortion, this argument works only if one *assumes* that the unborn are not human persons. For if they are human persons, then such a policy would justify numerous bizarre choices. Would the killing of three year olds be morally acceptable if it would eliminate the abuse of five year olds? What morally distinguishes the unborn from the infant, the three year old or the five year old? The real question is *not* "Does abortion curb child abuse?" but "Are the unborn human persons?" After all, if the unborn are human persons, then abortion is the worst sort of child abuse imaginable.

Second, it is not factually correct to say that "uwantedness" is responsible for child abuse. Professor Stephen Krason found in his research that "the factors causing child abuse cited most frequently by researchers are not 'unwantedness,' but parents' lack of social support from family, friends, and community; hostility toward them by society based on a disapproved sexual and social pattern of existence; and most commonly, their having been abused and neglected themselves when they were children."[6]

Third, the "unwantedness" of children tells us a great deal about our psychological and moral make-up, but very little about the child involved. It is a self-centered people who do not consider it a self-evident obligation to care for the most vulnerable and defenseless members of the human community. A lack of caring is a flaw in the one who ought to care, not in the person who ought to be cared for. Therefore, whether or not abortion is morally justified depends on whether the unborn are human persons, not on whether they are wanted.

> A lack of caring is a flaw in the one who ought to care, not in the person who ought to be cared for.

Fourth, the argument from child abuse is irrelevant to establishing abortion rights. Think about it. Imagine if everyone, including abortion advocates, admitted that there was no correlation between access to abortion and reducing child abuse. Would the defender of abortion rights then abandon his viewpoint because of this information? Of course not. For, as we saw in Lesson 2, the legal right to abortion is based on a woman's *right to choose*, unencumbered by government and spousal interference, and *not* on whether the reasons for that choice are good, bad, or indifferent. For this reason, it is a mystery why abortion advocates use this argument, since its plausibility has no bearing on whether a woman has or does not have a legal and/or moral right to abortion.

ARGUMENT FROM POVERTY

Some defenders of abortion rights maintain that abortion is a good thing to permit and promote because it is a way to help poor families avoid the financial and emotional burden a new child may put on them.

This argument is morally and logically bankrupt, because, like the other arguments we have covered, it also begs the question. That is, only if the abortion advocate assumes that the unborn poor are not human persons does his policy carry any weight. For if the unborn poor are human persons, abortion as a means to eliminate poverty is grossly immoral. It is tantamount to saying that the best way to eliminate poverty is to exterminate the poor.

ARGUMENT FROM RAPE AND INCEST

A woman or young girl who becomes pregnant because of rape or incest is the victim of a violent and reprehensible crime. Although pregnancy due to rape or incest is extremely rare, it does happen. Bioethicist Andrew Varga, an opponent of abortion, summarizes the argument from rape and incest:

> It is argued that in these tragic cases the great value of the mental health of a woman who becomes pregnant as a result of rape or incest can best be safe-guarded by abortion. It is

also said that a pregnancy caused by rape or incest is the result of a grave injustice and that the victim should not be obliged to carry the fetus to viability. This would keep reminding her for nine months of the violence committed against her and would just increase her mental anguish. It is reasoned that the value of the woman's mental health is greater than the value of the fetus. In addition, it is maintained that the fetus is an aggressor against the woman's integrity and personal life; it is only just and morally defensible to repel an aggressor even by killing him if that is the only way to defend personal and human values. It is concluded, then, that abortion is justified in these cases.[7]

This argument is flawed for several reasons. First, it is not adequate to support the abortion rights position, a position that affirms a right to abort at any time and for any reason — convenience, poverty, rape, etc. Arguing for the right to abortion from the narrow cases of rape and incest is like trying to argue for the elimination of traffic laws from the fact that one might need to violate some laws in rare circumstances, such as when one's spouse or child needs to be rushed to the hospital. So even if abortion were justified in cases of rape and incest, this would not mean that there is a general right to abortion in all circumstances throughout pregnancy.

Second, the unborn is not an aggressor when its presence does not endanger her mother's life. It is the rapist who is the aggressor. The unborn is just as much an innocent victim as her mother.

Third, this argument, like so many other arguments for abortion rights, begs the question by *assuming* the unborn is not a human person. For if the unborn is a human person, then this argument is saying

> The unborn is just as much an innocent victim as her mother.

that it is permissible to kill an innocent human person if one believes it may relieve another of mental anguish. But homicide is never justified to relieve emotional distress. After all, the unborn who is not a product of rape is biologically and morally indistinguishable from the unborn who results from rape or incest.

If the unborn is a human person (which is the *real* question), to request that its life be forfeited for the alleged benefit of another is to violate a basic principle of ethics: "we may never kill innocent person B to save person A." For example, "we cannot kill John by removing a vital organ in order to save Mary, who needs it. This is not a lack of compassion for Mary; it is the refusal to commit murder, even for a good cause. John has a right not to be killed to benefit Mary, even to save her life. Mary has the same right. We could not kill the woman to benefit the child. Equally, we cannot kill the child to benefit the woman." In abortion, "the child is being sacrificed for the benefit of another. He has no duty to do this; it is not right to force him. Would those who favor abortion for rape volunteer their lives so that another may be benefited in a similar way? If not, is it right to force this on another person? If yes, at least they have the opportunity to make

> To refuse to commit murder, even for a good cause, is not a lack of compassion.

a choice; the child does not?"[8] Simply because some people believe that the unborn's death may result in the happiness of another does not mean that she has a duty to die.

ARGUMENT FROM TOLERANCE

In an attempt to maintain an apparently "neutral" posture on the question of the unborn's personhood, abortion advocates sometimes argue in the following way: because people disagree about abortion, we ought to simply permit each person to decide for himself or herself whether the unborn is a human person and/or whether abortion is immoral. Consequently, if pro-lifers believe that abortion is homicide, that is fine. They need not fear state coercion to have an abortion or to participate in the procedure. On the other hand, if some people believe that abortion is not homicide and/or it is morally permissible, then they need not fear state coercion to remain pregnant. This, according to conventional wisdom, is the tolerant position one ought to take in our pluralistic society.

The problem with this reasoning is that it misses the point of why people oppose abortion. It does not seriously engage the opposition's case. Perhaps an example will help. During the 1984 U.S. presidential campaign when questions of Geraldine Ferraro's Catholicism[9] and its apparent conflict with her proabortion stance were prominent in the media, then New York Governor Mario Cuomo, in a lecture delivered at the University of Notre Dame, attempted to give the tolerance argument intellectual respectability.[10] He tried to provide a philosophical foundation for Ferraro's position. But Cuomo did not succeed. For one cannot appeal to the fact that we live in a pluralistic society, as Cuomo argued, when the very question of *who* is part of that society (that is, whether or not it includes the unborn) is itself the point under dispute. Cuomo lost the argument because he begged the question.

To tell pro-lifers, as supporters of the tolerance argument do, that "they have a right to believe what they want to believe" is evidence of a failure to truly grasp the pro-life perspective. Think about it. If *you* believed, as the pro-lifers do, that a class of persons were being unjustly killed by methods which include dismemberment, suffocation, brain-suctioning, and burning, wouldn't you be perplexed if someone tried to ease your outrage by telling you that you didn't have to participate in the killings if you didn't want to? That's exactly what pro-lifers hear when abortion advocates tell them "Don't like abortion, don't have one" or "I'm pro-choice, but personally opposed." In the mind of the pro-lifer, this is like telling an abolitionist, "Don't like slavery, don't own one," or telling Dietrich Bonhoeffer, "Don't like the Holocaust, don't kill a Jew." Consequently, for the defender of the tolerance argument to request that pro-lifers "should not force their pro-life belief on others," while claiming that "pro-lifers have a right to believe what they want to believe," is to reveal a gross misunderstanding of the pro-life position. Keep in mind that for the pro-lifer, an unborn child is no less a member of the human com-

> The tolerance argument is not as neutral as its proponents believe.

munity simply because she happens to be living inside Whoopi Goldberg, Eleanor Smeal, Kate Michelman, or any other abortion advocate. All the unborn deserve protection, even if they happen to reside in the wombs of citizens who do not embrace the pro-life viewpoint.

It seems, then, that the tolerance argument is not as neutral as its proponents believe. For to say that a woman should have the "right to choose" to terminate the life of the unborn human she is carrying is tantamount to denying the pro-life position that the unborn are human persons worthy of protection. And to affirm that the unborn are human persons with a "right to life" that ought to be protected by the state is tantamount to denying the proabortion position that a woman has a fundamental right to terminate her pregnancy, since such a termination would result in a homicide. Consequently, when abortion advocates, in the name of tolerance and pluralism, call for pro-life citizens to cease trying to protect the unborn, they are calling for pro-lifers to acquiesce to the legal status quo, namely, that the unborn are not full-fledged members of the human community and therefore are not entitled to protection by the state. To the pro-lifer, this request hardly seems neutral or tolerant.

PERSONAL ATTACKS ON PRO-LIFERS

Instead of dealing with the most important question in the abortion debate — Are the unborn human persons? — some defenders of abortion rights would rather attack pro-lifers and their motives. This

> Some defenders of abortion rights would rather attack pro-lifers and their motives.

tactic, though popular, is hopelessly flawed. Consider the following letter from a Dear Abby column:

> **Dear Abby:** This is a message to those men and women who try to prevent women from entering abortion clinics and carry big signs that say "They Kill Babies Here!"
> Have you signed up to adopt a child? If not, why not? Is it because you don't want one, can't afford one or don't have the time, patience or desire to raise a child?
> What if a woman who was about to enter a family planning clinic saw your sign, then decided not to have an abortion but chose to give her baby to you? Would you accept it? What if the mother belonged to a minority group — or was addicted to drugs, or tested positive for AIDS? . . .
> So, to those carrying those signs and trying to prevent

women from entering family planning clinics, heed my message: If you must be against abortion, don't be a hypocrite — make your time and energy count.[11]

This argument can be distilled into the following assertion: unless the pro-life advocate is willing to help bring up the children she does not want aborted, she has no right to prevent a woman from having an abortion. As a principle of moral action, this seems to be a rather bizarre assertion. It begs the question by *assuming* that the unborn are *not* human persons. Wouldn't we consider the murder of a couple's children unjustified even if we were approached by the parents with the ultimatum, "Unless you adopt our three children by noon tomorrow, we will put them to death"? The fact that we may refuse to adopt these children does not mean that their parents are justified in killing them. The issue, once more, is whether the unborn are human persons.

The unborn do not suddenly become nonpersons because individual pro-lifers are not currently involved in works of mercy.

Although the pro-life movement does have a moral duty to help those in need, especially unwed mothers (and there are enough organizations dedicated to this ministry to show that the pro-lifers do practice what they preach,[12]) the point I am making is that the unborn do not suddenly become nonpersons and not entitled to protection simply because individual pro-lifers are not currently involved in works of mercy.

Personal attacks against pro-lifers are attempts to avoid the question of whether the unborn are human persons. Although it is tempting to directly reply to such personal attacks, we should not do so. We should simply remind our attackers that such assaults have no bearing on the question of whether or not abortion is unjustified homicide. If they continue to refuse to engage in mature and serious dialogue on that question, then perhaps it is best to move on.

ARGUMENT FROM FETAL VIABILITY

The argument from fetal viability is another popular argument that is used to defend the right to abortion in the first two trimesters of pregnancy. Viability is the time at which the unborn can live outside her mother's womb (with or without the assistance of artificial life support). Some people have argued that since the unborn in the first two trimesters cannot survive independent of its mother, it is not a complete, independent human life and hence not a human person. Thus, prior to viability, abortion ought to remain legal.

There are several problems with this argument. First, because viability is a measure of the sophistication of our neonatal life-support systems, the preborn human being remains the same while viability changes. Viability measures medical technology, not one's humanity. For this reason, the viability criterion seems to be arbitrary and not applicable to the question of whether the unborn is a human person.

Second, because viability is contingent upon our medical technology, it would seem to follow,

> It is absurd to imply that a child born at 22-weeks gestation in 2000 is a human person while a 30-week unborn child in 1900 was not.

according to the viability argument, that a child born at 22-weeks gestation in 2000 is a human person while a 30-week unborn child in 1900 is not a human person. This is absurd.

Third, one could argue that the nonviability of the unborn, and the dependence and vulnerability that goes with that status, would lead one to have *more* rather than less concern for that being. Since when is a human being's dependence and vulnerability a *justification* to kill her rather than a call for her parents, family and the wider human community to care and nurture her?

Fourth, each of us, including the unborn, is nonviable in relation to his environment. If any one of us were to be placed naked on the moon or the earth's North Pole, one would quickly become aware of one's nonviability. Therefore, the unborn entity prior to the time she can live outside her mother's womb is as nonviable in relation to her environment as we are nonviable in relation to ours.

THE "LIFE OF THE MOTHER" EXCEPTION

Is abortion justified when continuing a pregnancy is likely to result in the death of the pregnant woman? I believe that the pro-life advocate can answer "yes" to this question without compromising her commitment to the sanctity of human life. Let me explain.

First, when pregnancy endangers a mother's life, medical personnel should try to save the lives of both mother and child.

Second, if that is not possible, the physician must choose the course of action which best upholds the sanctity of human life. Since it is the mother's body which serves as the environment in which the unborn is nurtured, it is impossible to save the unborn child before viability (roughly 20 to 24 weeks after conception).

In fact, almost all abortions performed to save the mother's life are done long before viability, since it is usually for an ectopic (or tubal) pregnancy. Consequently, in such cases, the physician must save the mother's life even if it results in the death of the unborn. His intention is not to kill the child but to save the mother. But since salvaging both is impossible, "abortion" to save the mother's life is justified.

> "When the woman is pregnant, her obstetrician takes on the care of two patients."

Third, after viability, when abortion itself is far riskier for the mother than is childbirth, there are very few if any instances in which an abortion will save the mother's life. But when such cases do occur, the same principles apply here as prior to viability. Former Surgeon General C. Everett Koop explains:

> When the woman is pregnant, her obstetrician takes on the care of two patients — the mother-to-be and the unborn baby. If, toward the end of the pregnancy, complications arise that threaten the mother's health, he will take the child by inducing labor or performing a Cesarean section.
>
> His intention is still to save the life of both the mother and the baby. The baby will be premature and perhaps immature depending on the length of gestation. Because it has suddenly been taken out of the protective womb, it may encounter threats to its survival. The baby is never willfully destroyed because the mother's life is in danger.[13]

Of course, if the unborn is *not* a human person, whether or not the pregnant woman's life is in danger is irrelevant. For abortion then would not be an act of homicide. It would be morally benign. If, however, the unborn is a human person, then abortion to save the mother's life is justified for the reasons given above.

These reasons are based on the pro-life ethic that life is sacred and that we should do our best to uphold that ethic, even if it means that a pregnancy should be terminated.

CONCLUSION

We saw in Lesson 1 that the most important question in the debate over abortion is "Are the unborn human persons?" In this lesson we saw that most of the leading popular arguments for abortion beg this fundamental question. For if the unborn is a human person, then these arguments collapse into irrelevancy. As Gregory P. Koukl puts it: "If the unborn is not a human person, no justificaiton for abortion is necessary. However, if the unborn is a human person, no justification is adequate."[14]

> Either no justification for abortion is needed, or no justification is sufficient.

NOTES

1. For more detailed replies to these and numerous other popular abortion rights arguments, see Francis J. Beckwith, *Politically Correct Death: Answering the Arguments for Abortion Rights* (Grand Rapids: Baker, 1993), chapters 4-7.

2. Mary Anne Warren, "On the Moral and Legal Status of Abortion," in *The Moral Problem of Abortion*, 2nd ed., ed. Joel Feinberg (Belmont, CA: Wadsworth, 1984), p. 103.

3. Mary Calderone, "Illegal Abortions as a Public Health Problem," *American Journal of Public Health* 50 (July 1960): 948-954.

4. See Laurence Lader, *Abortion* (Indianapolis: Bobbs-Merrill, 1966), p. 3; and Bernard Nathanson (with Richard Ostling), *Aborting America* (New York: Doubleday, 1979), p. 193; and Sally Quinn, "Our Choices, Our Selves," *Las Vegas Review-Journal* (14 April 1992): 9B.

5. Faye Wattleton, circular letter to members of Congress, 22 January 1979, as cited in Robert Marshall and Charles Donovan, *Blessed Are the Barren: The Social Policy of Planned Parenthood* (San Francisco: Ignatius, 1991), p. 262.

6. Stephen M. Krason, *Abortion: Politics, Morality, and the Constitution* (Lanham, MD: University Press of America, 1984), p. 320.

7. Andrew Varga, *The Main Issues in Bioethics*, rev. ed. (New York: Paulist Press, 1984), pp. 67-68.

8. Stephen D. Schwarz, *The Moral Question of Abortion* (Chicago: Loyola University Press, 1990), pp. 146, 151.

9. Ferraro was the vice-presidential candidate for the Democratic Party. Walter Mondale was the party's presidential candidate.

10. Mario Cuomo's talk was published as "Religious Belief and Public Morality," *Notre Dame Journal of Law, Ethics, and Public Policy* 1 (1984).

11. "Abortion Foes Challenged to Help," in *Dear Abby* column, in *Las Vegas Review-Journal* (October 4, 1989): 4f.

12. Among the many organizations are CareNet, Christian Action Council, and the hundreds of Crisis Pregancy Centers throughout North America.

13. C. Everett Koop, "Deception on Demand," *Moody Monthly* 80 (May, 1980): 26.

14. Gregory P. Koukl, *Precious Unborn Human Persons* (San Pedro, CA: Stand to Reason, 1999), p. 4.

Reflecting on Lesson Four

1. Present and discuss some of the popular arguments for abortion rights. Why do you think they are so persuasive to some people?

2. Why is the status of the unborn key to responding to the proabortion arguments covered in this lesson?

3. Can you think of some creative ways by which you can teach people that the popular arguments for the right to abortion are flawed? Are there some stories, analogies, or examples that you have thought of that others may find helpful?

4. What are some arguments for the right to abortion that we did not go over in this lesson? Critically evaluate those arguments in the same way that we analyzed the arguments in this lesson.

5. Why is the "life of the mother" exception consistent with the pro-life ethic?

Consider this:

What is a person? How do you define the terms "human" and "person"? Do you see a distinction between the two? If there is or is not a difference, how does this affect the debate over abortion? Be prepared to consider this issue in the next lesson.

5

PHILOSOPHERS
AGAINST THE FETUS

In this lesson:

▶ Attempted distinction between humanity and personhood
▶ Difference between human *being* and human *function*

"To be or not to be. That is the question."

—William Shakespeare *Hamlet* (1602)

"A person is a person no matter how small."

—Dr. Seuss, *Horton Hears a Who* (1954)

Given the clear and convincing evidence of the unborn's humanity (Lesson 2) and the failure of popular arguments to support a right to abortion (Lesson 4), abortion advocates are forced to defend their viewpoint by employing arguments that the ordinary citizen may have never entertained or thought possible. Nevertheless, these arguments have had a tremendous influence in the areas of medical ethics, moral philosophy, political theory, and theology. They have also found their way to a number of internet web sites and newsgroups.

In this lesson we will critically look at the position of those who say that the unborn, though a human being, is not a full-fledged member of the human community. In the next lesson we will examine an argument that tries to show that abortion is justified *even if* the unborn is a human person.

NOT ALL HUMAN BEINGS ARE PERSONS?

As we saw in Lesson 2, there is no doubt scientifically that individual human life begins at conception and does not end until natural death. At the moment of conception, when sperm and ovum cease to exist as individual entities, a new being with its own genetic

> There is no doubt scientifically that individual human life begins at conception and does not end until natural death.

code comes into existence. No new genetic information is added to the individual from this moment until natural death. All that is needed for its development is food, water, air, and an environment conducive to its survival.

These facts typically are not denied by those who believe that abortion should be justified at some point during pregnancy. What they argue is that the unborn, though a human being from conception, is not a person until some decisive moment after conception. Some argue that personhood does not arrive until brain waves are detected (40 to 43 days).[1] Others, such as Mary Anne Warren,[2] define a person as a being who can do certain things, such as have consciousness, solve complex problems, have a self-concept, and engage in sophisticated communication, which would put the arrival of personhood *after birth*. Still others, such as L.W. Sumner,[3] argue that human personhood does not arrive until the fetus is *sentient*, the ability to feel and sense as a conscious being. This, according to Sumner, occurs possibly as early as the middle weeks of the second trimester of pregnancy and definitely by the end of that trimester.

All these criteria have one thing in common: they assume that only if an entity *functions* in a certain way is it really a person. That is to say, defenders of these criteria argue that once the unborn acquires a

> Some argue that personhood does not arrive until brain waves are detected, or the individual has a conscious self-concept, or until the fetus is sentient.

certain function or functions — whether it is brain waves, rationality, sentience, etc. — it is then and only then that a person actually exists who deserves our respect and care. Those who defend these personhood criteria typically make a distinction between "being a human" and "being a person." They argue that although the unborn are part of the species *homo sapiens*, and in that sense are human, they are not truly persons since they fail to fulfill a particular set of personhood criteria.

PROBLEMS WITH PERSONHOOD CRITERIA

Although functional definitions of personhood may tell us some conditions that are sufficient to say that a being is a person, they are not adequate in revealing to us all the conditions that are sufficient for a particular being to be called a person. For example, when a person is asleep, unconscious, or temporarily comatose, she is not functioning as a person as defined by many personhood criteria. Nevertheless, no reasonable person would say that a human being is not a person while in any of these states. Consequently, to accept a functional definition of personhood one not only excludes the unborn, but also the unconscious, the temporarily comatose, and the sleeping. Therefore, it seems more consistent with our moral intuitions to say that a person functions as a person *because* she *is* a person and *not because* she *functions* as a person. That is, personhood is not something that arises when certain functions are in place, but rather is something that grounds these functions whether or not they are ever actualized in the life of a human being. Thus defining personhood strictly in terms of function is inadequate.

> A person functions as a person *because* she *is* a person, not the other way around.

The abortion advocate, in response, may want to argue that the analogy between sleeping/unconscious/comatose persons and the unborn breaks down because the former *at one time* in their existence functioned as persons and will probably do so in the future, while the latter, the unborn, did not. But this point seems to ignore the significant flaw in defining personhood strictly in terms of function; for to claim that a person can be functional, become nonfunctional, and then return to a state of function is to assume that there is some underlying personal unity to this individual which makes it intelligible for us to say that the person who has returned to functional capacity is the same person who was functional prior to being in a nonfunctional state and yet

> When a coma victim becomes functional again, has a *new person* suddenly popped into existence?

continued to exist while not functioning. If not, then we would have to make the absurd claim that a new "person" has popped into existence and that the original "person" ceased to exist upon the cessation of his personhood functions. If, however, we were to identify both the first person and the second person with the living human being from which these personal functions have arisen, then the human person *is* the human being as long as the human being exists.

Consider the following example. Suppose your Uncle Jed is in a terrible car accident that results in his being in a coma from which he may or may not wake. Imagine that he remains in this state for roughly two years and then awakens. He seems to be the same Uncle Jed that you knew before he went into the coma, even though he's lost some weight, hair, and memories. Was he a person during the coma? Could the physicians have killed Uncle Jed's body during that time because he was not functioning as a person? If one holds to the personhood criteria we reviewed above, it is difficult to see why it would be wrong to kill Uncle Jed while he is in the coma. Yet, it *would be* morally wrong to kill Uncle Jed while in this state.

You may be tempted to say that Uncle Jed's life while in the coma was valuable because *at one time* prior to the coma he

> If personhood is based solely on function, it is difficult to see why it would be wrong to kill someone who is in a coma.

functioned as a person and probably will do so in the future after coming out of the coma. But this would be a mistake, for we can change the story a bit and say that when Uncle Jed awakens from the coma he loses virtually all his memories and knowledge including his ability to speak a language, engage in rational thought, and have a self-concept. He then would be in the exact same position as the standard fetus, for he would have the same capacities as the fetus. He would still literally be the same person he was before the coma, but he would be more like he was before he had a "past." He would have the natural inherent capacity to speak a language, engage in rational thought, and have a self-concept, but he would have to develop and learn them all over again in order for these capacities to result, as they did before, in actual abilities.

Consider one more illustration. Imagine that there are two newborn twins, Larry and Ervin. Larry attains self-consciousness and then lapses into a coma for eight years, after which he will come out. Ervin is born in a coma, never attaining self-consciousness, and will come out of it the same moment as Larry. The only difference between Larry and Ervin is one of function — the former attained self-consciousness whereas the latter did not. Suppose one argues that it is permissible to kill Ervin but not Larry the day before they are set to come out of the coma. But this seems absurd. The difference between Larry and Ervin is functional only, not a difference in essence or nature, and thus not morally relevant, precisely the same kind of difference between the fetus and the five-year old. So, the unborn are not potential persons, but human persons with great potential.[4] Consequently, what is crucial morally is the *being* of a person, not his or her functioning.

A human person does not come into existence when human function arises, but rather, a human person is an entity who has the natural inherent capacity to give rise to human functions, whether or not those functions are ever attained. And since the unborn human being has this natural inherent capacity from the moment of coming into existence, she is a person as long as she exists. As John Jefferson Davis writes, "Our ability to have conscious experiences and recollections arises out of our personhood; the basic metaphysical reality of personhood precedes the unfolding of the conscious abilities inherent in it."[5]

> Since the unborn human being has natural inherent capacity to function in a human way from the moment of coming into existence, she is a person as long as she exists.

Philosopher J.P. Moreland clarifies this notion when he points out that "it is because an entity has an essence and falls within a natural kind that it can possess a unity of dispositions, capacities, parts and properties at a given time and can maintain identity through change." Moreover, "it is the natural kind that determines what kinds of activities are appropriate and natural for that entity."[6] Moreland goes on to write:

> . . . [A]n organism . . . has second-order capacities to have first-order capacities that may or may not obtain (through some sort of lack). These second-order capacities are grounded in the nature of the organism. For example, a child may not

have the first-order capacity to speak English due to a lack of education. But because the child has humanness it has the capacity to develop the capacity to speak English. The very idea of a defect presupposes these second-order capacities.

Now the natural kind "human being" or "human person" (I do not distinguish between these) is not to be understood as a mere biological concept. It is a metaphysical concept that grounds both biological functions and moral intuitions. . . .

In sum, if we ask why [certain functions are] . . . both possible and morally important, the answer will be that such [functions are] . . . grounded in the kind of entity, a human person in this case, that typically can have [those functions] . . . .[7]

What does Moreland mean by this? First, each kind of living organism, or *substance*, has a nature or essence that makes certain activities and functions possible. For example, a German Shepherd dog, because it has a particular nature, has the capacity to develop the ability to bark, even if it lacks the physical structure to practice it (i.e., mature vocal chords). It may die as a puppy and never develop that ability. Regardless, it is *still* a German Shepherd dog as long as it exists, because it possesses a particular nature, even if it never acquires certain functions that by nature it has the capacity to develop. In contrast, a frog is not said to lack something if it cannot bark, for it is by nature not the sort of being that can have the ability to bark. A dog that lacks the ability to bark *is still a dog* because of its nature. A human person who lacks the ability to think rationally (either because she is too young or she suffers from a disability) *is still a human person* because of her

A human being's lack makes sense *if and only if* she is an actual person.

nature. Consequently, a human being's lack makes sense *if and only if* she is an actual person.

As Stephen Schwarz writes: "The very existence and meaning of functioning as a person can have its basis only in the being of a person." In other words, "it is because you have the being of a person that you can function as a person, although you might fail to function as a person and still retain your full being as a person."[8]

Second, the German Shepherd remains the same particular German Shepherd over time from the moment it comes into existence. Suppose you buy this German Shepherd as a puppy and name her "Shannon." When you first bring her home, you notice that she is tiny in comparison to her parents and lacks their intellectual and physical abilities. But over time Shannon develops these abilities, learns a number of things her parents never learned, sheds her hair, has her nails clipped, becomes ten times larger than she was as a puppy, and undergoes significant development of her cellular structure, brain and cerebral cortex.

> Living organisms maintain identity through change.

Yet, this grown-up Shannon is identical to the puppy Shannon, even though it has gone through significant physical changes Why? Because living organisms (or "substances," as some philosophers like to call them) maintain identity through change. If not, then you never were literally a teenager, ten year old, three year old, infant, or newborn. But you know that you were, even though the physical differences between you as an infant and you as an adult are considerable. In fact, this same *you* was also once a fetus, an embryo, and a zygote. To be sure, you *have* changed. (When you go to your 20-year high school reunion, you'll really know who has changed!) But it is *you* who has changed. That's the important thing to understand. *You* remain *you* through all the changes. Thus, if you are a vaiuable human person now, then you were a valuable human person at *every moment in your past* including when you were in your mother's womb.

AN OBJECTION TO OUR CRITIQUE

Suppose the abortion rights advocate, in response to our case, denies that you remain the same human being through all the changes you apparently undergo through your life. Proponents of this view believe that a human being is a collection of parts, like a car or a computer. Such things are called *property-things*. So, like a computer or car, whose parts are replaced over time and is literally not the same computer or car it was when you first brought it home, a human being, because he loses and gains parts (like hair or brain tissue), is literally not the same human being from one moment to the next. Thus, according to this view, when a 45-year old prolifer says that she is the same human being that was the fetus her mother was carrying 45 and one-half years ago, the prolifer is mistaken. This is because the defender of this view believes that like a computer or car, there is no underlying *substance* that is *you* that endures through all the changes of your life. For if there were, then abortion would be homicide, because if you have a right to life *now* as an adult you would have had a right to life *then* as a fetus because you would be identical to your fetal self. What can we say in response to this viewpoint?[9]

First, human beings do not seem to resemble property-things like computers and cars in any significant way. A human being seems to have an internal essence or nature that directs the development of its parts, while a property-thing seems not to have an internal essence or nature, and thus is only changed externally and its parts have no power to arrange or rearrange themselves. Think about it: a human being, from conception, grows and develops certain functions, organs, and attributes as a result of what it is, what it is internally directed to do by its *nature*, while a car or a computer will be built only when its parts are put together and ordered by an outside mind, and even then it will just sit there unless manipulated by something external to itself. A human being, unlike a computer or car, is *prior to* its parts, for its parts function as a result of the nature of the human organism itself. A human being *has* parts while a car or computer *is* parts. This is why a human being maintains absolute identity through change while a computer or car does not.

> A human being, unlike a computer or car, is *prior to* its parts

Second, each of us has first person awareness of himself or herself as a unified and enduring self over time. As Moreland points out, "Our knowledge that we are first person substantial, unified, enduring selves that have bodies and mental states but are not identical to them is grounded in our awareness of ourselves."[10] This is why, for example, I may fear punishment in the future for deeds I committed years ago, discuss my infancy with my parents, recall a time when I lost consciousness, have regrets for decisions in the past I ought not to have made, look back fondly on my childhood, and reflect upon what I have accomplished and whether I have fulfilled my potential. In other words,

I *know* that I am an *I* that endures throughout all the changes of my life. "It is hard to see what kind of knowledge could be more certain than this. . . ."[11]

Third, a human action involves thinking, reflection, deliberation, actualizing an intention, and bodily movement over time, such as when one proposes and carries out a play in a basketball game or attends a four-year college and graduates. But if a human being is merely a property-thing, then there is no substantial self that remains the same, that endures, through the entire human action. In other words, the person thinking literally would be a different person than the ones reflecting, deliberating, actualizing an intention and engaging in bodily movement. To use a concrete example, the Michael Jordan who decides to shoot the basketball is literally not the same Michael Jordan who actually shoots the basketball. But this seems absurd.

Fourth, most abortion rights advocates believe that human beings have unchanging natural rights that they possess as long as they are persons. But if there is no substantial self that endures over time, then how can a human person possess these rights over the entirety of her life if the human person has no nature or essence and does not literally endure as the same self over the entirety of her life? In other words, if there is no enduring *who*, then to whom does the property of unchanging natural rights belong? A collection of parts, a property-thing, we merely call "human person" out of linguistic convention? That hardly seems right, for property-things

> If there is no continuity of self, the Michael Jordan who decides to shoot the basketball is not the same Michael Jordan who actually shoots the basketball.

are not substances with natures and therefore cannot have natural rights. So, if one is committed to unchanging natural rights, one must believe that human persons are enduring substances.

Suppose that the abortion rights advocate responds to the above four points in the following way: one does not have to believe in an enduring self, for one can just as well believe that a "person" consists of a string of psychological experiences over time connected by memory, beliefs, and/or character. Just as the Chicago Bulls of 1980 are connected to the Chicago Bulls of 2000 by a certain continuity of players, ownership, league membership, management, and location, even though each has slowly changed little by little over time, the "self" is connected psychologically in the same way by a continuity of memory, beliefs, and/or character, even though each slowly changes little by little over time. Just as there does not have to be an unchanging substance called "Chicago Bulls" there does not have be a substantial human self that endures through the changes it undergoes over time. There are at least three problems with this response.

First, it does not really address the objections raised above. It merely offers an alternative explanation that is not as good as just believing that there exists an enduring self. After all, it does seem that human beings are not like cars or computers (or the Chicago Bulls), that I do have first person awareness of myself as an enduring and unified substance over time, that I endure as the same self throughout the process of my acting, and that I have unchanging natural rights by virtue of being a living substance with a human nature.

Second, if human beings do not maintain absolute identity over time because a human person is merely a string of psychological experiences connected by memory, beliefs, and/or character, then it would be morally permissible to kill certain human beings that are clearly persons. Take for example, again, your Uncle Jed. Suppose that while in the coma his physician tells you that Uncle Jed will come out of the coma, but when he comes out he will not have any of the memories, beliefs, or knowledge that he once possessed, though he may be able to regain them over the years following his recovery through the normal process of learning. In essence, Uncle Jed would be, while in the coma, in

Uncle Jed would be, while in the coma, in the same position as the standard fetus.

the same position as the standard fetus. But it seems that according to the abortion rights advocate it would be permissible to kill Uncle Jed while he is in the coma, for while in that state he would not be part of a string of psychological experiences connected by memory, beliefs, and/or character. Yet, that seems wrong, for it seems correct to say that Uncle Jed in the coma, before the coma, and during the coma is the same Uncle Jed, that he maintains absolute identity through change. Thus, killing Uncle Jed while in the coma would be an act of homicide. So, if we identify both Uncle Jed before the coma and Uncle Jed after the coma with Uncle Jed during the coma, then the human person *is* the living human being as long as he exists. There are, therefore, no such things as living human beings that are not persons.

Third, if human persons are merely a string of psychological experiences connected by memory, beliefs, and/or character, then infants and newborns are not persons, for their psychological lives have not reached that level of complexity. However, it seems that infants and newborns are human persons. So, the abortion rights advocate must be mistaken on what counts as a person. Of course, some abortion rights advocates, such as Peter

Singer,[12] bite the bullet on this point and say that newborns and infants are in fact not persons and that infanticide is morally permissible. For some people, that is reason enough to reject the position, though we have provided in this lesson a number of other reasons as well.

It is clear that the substance view, that human beings are human persons as long as they exist, in comparison to the property-thing view, better accounts for our common sense intuitions about personal identity and moral obligation.

CONCLUSION

Because the functions of personhood are grounded in the essential nature of human personhood and because human beings are persons that maintain identity through change, it follows that the unborn are human persons of great worth because they possess that nature as long as they exist. No doubt much more can be said about the problem of what constitutes personhood,[13] but what is important to understand is that so-called personhood criteria are riddled with serious problems and that the pro-life advocate has been given no compelling reason to abandon her belief that the unborn are full-fledged members of the human community.

NOTES

1. See Baruch Brody, *Abortion and the Sanctity of Human Life: A Philosophical View* (Cambridge, MA: MIT Press, 1975).

2. See Mary Anne Warren, "On the Moral and Legal Status of Abortion," in *The Problem of Abortion*, 2nd ed., ed. Joel Feinberg (Belmont, CA: Wadsworth, 1984).

3. See L.W. Sumner, *Abortion and Moral Theory* (Princeton, NJ: Princeton University Press, 1981).

4. Stephen Schwarz provides a similar analogy in *The Moral Question of Abortion* (Chicago: Loyola University Press, 1990), p. 90.

5. John Jefferson Davis, *Abortion and the Christian* (Phillipsburg, NJ: Presbyterian & Reformed, 1984), p. 57.

6. J.P. Moreland, "James Rachels and the Active Euthanasia Debate," *Journal of the Evangelical Theological Society* 31 (March, 1988): 86.

7. Ibid., 87. For a fuller defense of this "substance" view of persons, see J.P. Moreland and Scott B. Rae, *Body and Soul* (Downers Grove, IL: Inter-Varsity Press, 2000).

8. Schwarz, *Moral Question*, p. 94.

9. For a response more detailed than I can offer here, see Patrick Lee, *Abortion and Unborn Human Life* (Washington, DC: The Catholic University of America Press, 1996), pp. 37-45; and Moreland and Rae, *Body and Soul*.

10. J.P. Moreland, "Humanness, Personhood, and the Right to Die," *Faith and Philosophy* 12.1 (January 1995), p. 103.

11. Ibid.

12. Peter Singer and Helga Kuhse admit that "prolife groups are right about one thing: the location of the baby inside or outside the womb cannot make such a crucial moral difference . . . . The solution, however, is not to accept the pro-life view that the fetus is a human being with the same moral standing as yours or mine. The solution is the very opposite: to abandon the idea that all human life is of equal worth." ("On Letting Handicapped Infants Die," in *The Right Thing to Do: Basic Readings in Moral Philosophy*, ed. James Rachels (New York: Random House, 1989), p. 146.

13. See the articles on personhood in *The Abortion Controversy 25 Years after Roe v. Wade: A Reader*, 2nd ed., eds. Louis P. Pojman and Francis J. Beckwith (Belmont, CA: Wadsworth, 1998).

Reflecting on Lesson Five

1. Why do some supporters of abortion rights distinguish human beings from human persons?

2. What are some of the personhood criteria that philosophers have defended and what do they all have in common?

3. Concerning the third flaw, why is functioning as a person inadequate in capturing what it means to be a human person?

4. What is the property-thing view of human beings, and why is it flawed?

Consider this:

Most "pro-choice" people will come back eventually to the argument "a woman has a right to do what she wants with her own body." As you prepare for the next lesson, consider how you would answer this argument.

6

ABORTION AND BODILY RIGHTS

In this lesson:

▶ The problem of using another person's body for life support
▶ Ethical responsibilities and choice
▶ The difference between active killing and withholding help
▶ Family law and responsibility
▶ The anti-feminist implications of bodily autonomy

"If a woman decides in the depth of her soul . . . that she doesn't want to have a child, then I think that's her right to say no, but let's not pretend that it isn't a form of killing."

—Norman Mailer

"So, what will it be: Wanted fetuses are charming, complex,
REM-dreaming beings whose profile on the sonogram looks just like
Daddy, but unwanted ones are mere 'uterine material'? How can we charge
that it is vile and repulsive for pro-lifers to brandish vile and repulsive
images if the images are real? To insist that the truth is in poor taste is the
very height of hypocrisy. Besides, if these images are the facts of the matter,
and if we then claim that it is offensive to pro-choice women to be confronted
by them, then we are making the judgment that women are too inherently
weak to face a truth about which they have to make a grave decision.
This view of women is unworthy of feminism.
Free women must be strong women, too; and strong women, presumably,
do not seek to cloak their most important decisions in euphemism."

—Naomi Wolf, feminist author

Some supporters of abortion rights do not believe that the
most important question to answer concerning the morality of
abortion is whether or not the unborn is a human person. They
argue that even if the unborn is a human person from conception or sometime early on in pregnancy, abortion is still morally
justified and, therefore, ought to remain legal.

Judith Jarvis Thomson, an emeritus professor of philosophy at
the Massachusetts Institute of Technology, argues that the
unborn's physical dependence on her mother's body entails a
conflict of rights if the pregnant
woman did not explicitly consent to become pregnant.[1] The
unborn, even if she is a human
person, cannot use her mother's body without her mother's
consent. Thus, a pregnant woman's expulsion of the unborn by
abortion, though it will result in the unborn's death, is no more
immoral than an adult's refusal to donate her kidney to someone

> The unborn has a
> physical dependence
> on her mother's body.

who needs one, though this refusal will probably result in the death of the person who needs the kidney. In order to make her point, Thomson employs what has since become one of the most well-known analogies in contemporary philosophy:

> You wake up in the morning and find yourself back to back in bed with an unconscious violinist. A famous unconscious violinist. He has been found to have a fatal kidney ailment, and the Society of Music Lovers has canvassed all the available medical records and found that you alone have the right blood type to help. They have therefore kidnapped you, and last night the violinist's circulatory system was plugged into yours, so that your kidneys can be used to extract poisons from his blood as well as your own. The director of the hospital now tells you, "Look we're sorry the Society of Music Lovers did this to you — we would never have permitted it if we had known. But still, they did it, and the violinist now is plugged into you. To unplug you would be to kill him. But never mind, it's only for nine months. By then he will have recovered from his ailment, and can safely be unplugged from you." Is it morally incumbent on you to accede to this situation? No doubt it would be very nice of you if you did, a great kindness. But do you have to accede to it? What if it were not nine months, but nine years? Or still longer? What if the director of the hospital says, "Tough luck, I agree, but you've now got to stay in bed, with the violinist plugged into you, for the rest of your life. Because remember this. All persons have a right to life, and violinists are persons. Granted you have a right to decide what happens in and to your body, but a person's right to life outweighs your right to decide what happens in and to your body. So you cannot ever be unplugged from him." I imagine that you would regard this as outrageous. . . .[2]

Thomson is asking "what happens if, for the sake of argument, we allow the premise that the unborn are fully human or persons. How, precisely, are we supposed to get from there to the conclusion that abortion is morally impermissible?"[3] To put it another way: assuming that the unborn is a human person, does that mean that it is *never* permissible to kill that person? Although ethicists maintain that it is *ordinarily* wrong to kill a human person, a vast majority agree that there may be some circumstances in which taking a human life or letting someone die is justified, such as in the cases of a just war, capital punishment, self-defense, or withdrawing medical

> Thomson argues that abortion should be included in those instances where killing is justified.

treatment. Thomson argues that abortion should be included as one of these justified circumstances. She maintains that because pregnancy constitutes an infringement by the unborn on the pregnant woman's personal bodily autonomy, the ordinary abortion is not wrong, even if it results in the death of a human person. Although there are a number of problems with Thomson's argument,[4] the following five are sufficient to reject it.

THOMSON ASSUMES ETHICAL VOLUNTEERISM.

If one were to use the violinist story as a model for all relationships between persons, one would have to conclude that all moral obligations must be voluntarily accepted in order to be legitimate. In other words, there are no moral obligations that are not the result of one volunteering for them. This would mean that obligations to one's infant offspring or to other vulnerable persons who need our care are merely voluntary as well. But this is clearly false. Consider the following story.

Suppose a couple has a sexual encounter which is fully protected by several forms of birth-control short of abortion (condom, the Pill, IUD, etc.), but nevertheless results in conception. Instead of getting an abortion, the mother of the unborn decides to bring it to term although the father is unaware of this decision. After the birth of the child the mother pleads with the father for child support. Because he refuses, she seeks legal action and takes him to court. Although he took every precaution to avoid fatherhood, thus showing that he did not wish to accept such a status, according to nearly all child support laws in the United States he would still be obligated to pay support *precisely because* of his relationship to this child.[5] As Michael Levin points out, "All child-support laws make the parental body an indirect resource for the child. If the father is a construction worker, the state will intervene unless some of his calories he expends lifting equipment go to providing food for his children."[6] For this reason, Keith Pavlischek, argues that "given the logic of" Thomson's argument, "the most reasonable course to follow would be to surrender the defense of paternal support laws for those children whose fathers would rather have had their children aborted," which "will lend some credence not only to the pro-life insistence on the corollary — that an intimate connection exists between the way we collectively relate to the unborn and the way we relate to our children after birth — but also to the claim made by pro-life feminists that the abortion mentality simply reaffirms the worst historical failings, neglect, and chauvinism of males."[7]

> A reluctant father's obligation to pay child support is precisely because of his relationship to the child.

THE UNBORN HAS A RIGHT TO HER MOTHER'S BODY.

Because there are moral obligations that do *not* have to be voluntarily accepted in order to be legitimate, it seems correct to say that the unborn, in ordinary circumstances, has a right to reside in her mother's body. There are at least three reasons to believe this is true.

(1) Unlike Thomson's violinist who is artificially attached to another person in order to save his life and is therefore not naturally dependent on any particular human being, the unborn is a human being who is by her very nature *dependent* on her mother, for this is how human beings are at this stage of their development.

(2) This period of a human being's *natural* development occurs in the womb. This is the journey which *we all* must take and is a necessary condition for *any* human being's postuterine existence. And this fact alone brings out the most glaring disanalogy between the violinist and the unborn: the womb is the unborn's natural environment whereas being artificially hooked-up to a stranger is not the natural environment for the violinist.

(3) This same entity, when it becomes a newborn, has a right to her parents' care, regardless of whether her parents "wanted" her. This is why we prosecute child-abusers, people who throw their babies in trash cans, and parents who abandon their children. Although it is true that pregnancy and childbirth entail certain emotional, physical, and financial sacrifices on the part of the pregnant woman, these sacrifices are also true of *parent-*

> The emotional and financial sacrifices of pregnancy are true of *parenthood* in general.

hood in general (which ordinarily lasts much longer than nine months), and do not justify the execution of troublesome infants and younger children who have a right to certain financial and bodily goods which are under the ownership of their parents. If the unborn is a human person, as Thomson is willing to grant, why should the unborn's right to her parents' goods differ before birth? Of course, a court will not force a parent to donate a kidney to her dying offspring, but this sort of dependence on the parent's body is highly unusual and is not part of the ordinary obligations associated with the *natural* process of human development, just as in the case of the violinist's artificial dependency on the reluctant music lover.

> There are ordinary obligations associated with the *natural* process of human development.

As Schwarz points out: "So, the very thing that makes it plausible to say that the person in bed with the violinist has no duty to sustain him; namely, that he is a stranger unnaturally hooked up to him, is precisely what is absent in the case of the mother and her child." That is to say, the mother "does have an obligation to take care of her child, to sustain her, to protect her, and especially, to let her live in the only place where she can now be protected, nourished, and allowed to grow, namely the womb."[8]

ABORTION IS KILLING AND NOT MERELY THE WITHHOLDING OF TREATMENT.

Thomson makes an excellent point in her use of the violinist story: there are times when withholding and/or withdrawing of medical treatment is morally justified. For instance, you are not morally obligated to donate your kidney to Fred, your next door neighbor, simply because he needs a kidney in order to live. In other words, you are not obligated to risk your life so that Fred may live a few years longer. Fred should not expect that of you. If, however, you donate one of your kidneys to Fred, you will have acted above and beyond the call of duty. But this case is not analogous to pregnancy and abortion.

Levin argues that there is an essential difference between abortion and the unplugging of the violinist. In the case of the violinist (as well as your relationship to Fred's welfare), "the person who withdraws [or withholds] his assistance is not completely responsible for the dependency on him of the person who is about to die, while the mother is completely responsible for the dependency of her fetus on her. When one is completely responsible for dependence, refusal to continue to aid is indeed killing." For example, "if a woman brings a newborn home from the hospital, puts it in its crib and refuses to feed it until it has starved to death, it would be absurd to say that she simply refused to assist it and had done nothing for which she should be criminally liable."[9] In other words, just as the withholding of food kills the child after birth, in the case of abortion it is the *abortion* which kills the child. In neither case is there any ailment from which the child suffers and which highly invasive medical treatment, with the cooperation of another's bodily organs, is necessary in order to cure this ailment and save the child's life.

Or consider the case of a man who finds a baby at his doorstep (like in the film with Tom Selleck, Ted Danson, and Steve Guttenberg, *Three Men and a Baby*). Suppose that no one else is able to take care of the child because the man lives on a deserted island and is incapable of contacting anyone, but according to a note attached to the child, the man only has to take care of the child for nine months after which a couple will arrive on the island and adopt the child. Would "withholding treatment" from this child and its subsequent death be justified on the basis that the homeowner did not ask for the child to appear on his doorstep and because the child's hasty death would relieve the homeowner of the burden of caring for the child for the entire nine months? Is any person, born or unborn, obligated to sacrifice his life because his death would benefit another person? Once the homeowner recognizes the newborn's natural vulnerability, utter helplessness, and need for adult care, he knows what humanity requires of him. To intentionally ignore this requirement is, in a word, evil. Thus, there is no doubt that such "withholding" of treatment (and it seems totally false to call ordinary shelter and sustenance "treatment") is indeed unjustified homicide.

But is it even accurate to refer to abortion as the "withholding of support or treatment?" Schwarz and R.K. Tacelli make the important point that although "a woman who has an abortion is indeed 'withholding support' from her unborn child. . . . abortion is far more than that. It is the active killing of a human person — by burning him, by crushing him, by dismembering him."[10] Euphemistically calling abortion the "withholding of support or treatment" makes about as much sense as calling suffocating someone with a pillow the withdrawing of oxygen.

THOMSON'S ARGUMENT IGNORES FAMILY LAW.

Thomson's argument is inconsistent with the body of well-established family law, which presupposes parental responsibility for a child's welfare. And, of course, assuming as Thomson does that the unborn are fully human, this body of law would also apply to parents'

> Family law presupposes parental responsibility for a child's welfare.

responsibility for their unborn children. According to legal scholars Dennis J. Horan and Burke J. Balch, "All 50 states, the District of Columbia, American Samoa, Guam, and the U.S. Virgin Islands have child abuse and neglect statutes which provide for the protection of a child who does not receive needed medical care." They further state that "a review of cases makes it clear that these statutes are properly applied to secure emergency medical treatment and sustenance (food or water, whether given orally or through intravenous or nasogastric tube) for children when parents, with or without the acquiescence of physicians, refuse to provide it."[11] Evidently, "pulling the plug" on a perfectly healthy unborn human being, assuming that it is a person, would clearly violate these statutes.

For example, in a case in New York, a court ruled that the parents' actions constituted neglect when they failed to provide medical care to a child with leukemia: "The parent . . . may not deprive a child of lifesaving treatment, however well-intentioned. Even when the parents' decision to decline necessary treatment is based on constitutional grounds, such as religious beliefs, it must yield to the State's interests, as parens patriae, in protecting the health and welfare of the child."[12] Horan and Balch conclude that the "courts have uniformly held that a parent has the legal responsibility of furnishing his dependent child with adequate food and medical care."[13]

It is evident then that child-protection laws reflect our deepest moral intuitions about parental and community responsibility and the utter helplessness of infants and small children.

THOMSON'S ARGUMENT IS ANTI-FEMINIST.

Even though Thomson's argument and ones similar to it are used by feminists to defend the right to abortion, some feminists have argued that these arguments are actually anti-feminist.[14] One feminist publication asks the question, "What kind of control are we talking about? A control that allows for violence against another human being is a macho, oppressive kind of control. Women rightly object when others try to have that kind of control over them, and the movement for women's rights asserts the moral right of women to be free from the control of others." After all, "abortion involves violence against a small, weak and dependent child. It is macho control, the very kind the feminist movement most eloquently opposes in other contexts."[15]

> "A control that allows for violence against another human being is a macho, oppressive kind of control."

Celia Wolf-Devine makes the observation that "abortion has something . . . in common with the behavior ecofeminists and pacifist feminists take to be characteristically masculine; it shows a willingness to use violence in order to take control. The fetus is destroyed by being pulled apart by suction, cut in pieces, or poisoned." Wolf-Devine goes on to point out that "in terms of social thought . . . it is the masculine models which are most frequently employed in thinking about abortion. If masculine thought is naturally hierarchical and oriented toward power and control, then the interests of the fetus (who has no power) would naturally be suppressed in favor of the interests of the mother. But to the extent that feminist social thought is egalitarian, the question must be raised of why the mother's interests should prevail over the child's. . . . Feminist thought about abortion has . . . been deeply pervaded by the individualism which they so ardently criticize."[16]

CONCLUSION

Thomson's attempt to avoid the question of the unborn's personhood is a failure. Her violinist analogy, though powerful, is seriously flawed. For if our society and courts were to embrace it as legitimate, it would help undermine the deep *natural bond* between mother and child by making it seem no different than two strangers artificially hooked-up to each other so that one can "steal" the service of the other's kidneys. Never has something so human, so natural, so beautiful, and so wonderfully demanding of our human creativity and love been reduced to such a brutal caricature.

NOTES

1. Judith Jarvis Thomson, "A Defense of Abortion," in *The Problem of Abortion*, 2nd ed., ed. Joel Feinberg (Belmont, CA: Wadsworth, 1984), pp. 173-187. This article was originally published in *Philosophy and Public Affairs* 1 (1971): 47-66. All references to Thomson's article in this paper are from the Feinberg book.

2. Thomson, "A Defense of Abortion," pp. 174-175.

3. Ibid., p. 174.

4. For more detailed critiques of Thomson's argument, see Baruch Brody, *Abortion and the Sanctity of Human Life: A Philosophical View* (Cambridge, MA: MIT Press, 1975), pp. 26-33; Doris Gordon, "Abortion and Rights: Applying Libertarian Principles Correctly." *Studies in Prolife Feminism* 1.2 (Spring 1995); and Francis J. Beckwith, "Arguments from Bodily Rights: A Critical Analysis" and Keith Pavlischek, "Abortion Logic and Paternal Responsibilities: One More Look at Judith Thomson's Argument and a Critique of David Boonin-Vail's Defense of It," in *The Abortion Controversy 25 Years after Roe v. Wade: A Reader*, 2nd ed.., ed. Louis P. Pojman and Francis J. Beckwith (Belmont, CA: Wadsworth, 1998). For defenses of Thomson's argument and ones similar to it, see Eileen McDonagh, *Breaking the Abortion Deadlock: From Choice to Consent* (New York: Oxford University Press, 1996); F.M. Kamm, *Creation and Abortion: A Study in Moral and Legal Philosophy* (New York: Oxford University Press, 1992); and David Boonin-Vail, "A Defense of `A Defense of Abortion': On the Responsibility Objection to Thomson's Argument," in *The Abortion Controversy.*

5. See *In the Best Interest of the Child: A Guide to State Child Support and Paternity Laws*, eds. Carolyn Royce Kastner and Lawrence R. Young (n.p.: Child Support Enforcement Beneficial Laws Project, National Conference of State Legislatures, 1981).

6. Michael Levin, review of *Life in the Balance* by Robert Wennberg, *Constitutional Commentary* 3 (Summer 1986): 511.

7. Keith J. Pavlischek, "Abortion Logic and Paternal Responsibilties: One More Look at Judith Thomson's 'A Defense of Abortion,'" *Public Affairs Quarterly* 7 (October 1993): 343. A revised version of this article appears in *The Abortion Controversy* (see note 4).

8. Schwarz, *The Moral Question of Abortion*, p. 118.

9. Michael Levin, *Feminism and Freedom* (New Brunswick, NJ: Transaction Books, 1987), pp. 288-289.

10. Stephen D. Schwarz and R.K. Tacelli, "Abortion and Some Philosophers: A Critical Examination," *Public Affairs Quarterly* 3 (April 1989): 85.

11. Dennis J. Horan and Burke J. Balch, *Infant Doe and Baby Jane Doe: Medical Treatment of the Handicapped Newborn*, Studies in Law & Medicine Series (Chicago: Americans United for Life, 1985), p. 2.

12. *In re Storar*, 53 N.Y. 2d 363, 380-381, 420 N.E. 2d 64, 73, 438 N.Y.S. 2d 2d 2d 266, 275 (1981), as quoted in ibid., pp. 2-3.

13. Horan and Balch, *Infant Doe*, pp. 3-4.

14. Although not dealing exclusively with Thomson's argument, Celia Wolf-Devine's article is quite helpful: "Abortion and the 'Feminine Voice,'" *Public Affairs Quarterly* 3 (July 1989). See, also, Sidney Callahan, "Abortion and the Sexual Agenda," *Commonweal* 113 (April 25, 1986); and Janet Smith, "Abortion as a Feminist Concern," in *The Zero People*, ed. Jeff Lane Hensley (Ann Arbor, MI: Servant, 1983). Wolf-Devine's essay is republished in *The Abortion Controversy*.

15. n.a., *Sound Advice for All Prolife Activists and Candidates Who Wish to Include a Concern for Women's Rights in Their Prolife Advocacy: Feminists for Life Debate Handbook* (Kansas City, MO: Feminists for Life of American, n.d.), pp. 15-16.

16. Wolf-Devine, "Abortion," pp. 86, 87.

Reflecting on Lesson Six

1. Present and explain Thomson's argument. Why and how does she challenge the claim that the most important question in the abortion debate is the nature of the unborn?

2. What are the flaws in Thomson's argument?

3. Suppose someone responds to our criticism of Thomson's argument in this way: "You're right that Thomson's argument doesn't work in most cases of abortion if we assume, like Thomson, that the unborn are human persons. However, why wouldn't the argument work in the case of rape?" How would you respond to this question?

4. Suppose that technology reaches a point at which the unborn from conception could be removed from their mothers' wombs and placed in artificial wombs without any risk to either the mother or the unborn. If this were possible, then pregnancy could be terminated without killing the unborn. How do you think Thomson would respond to this possibility? Would she say that the mother has a right to the death of the unborn? Why or why not?

Consider this:

For the Christian, biblical teaching is as important as all the legal and philosophical arguments put together. Try to have a list of Scriptures ready next time that deal with the abortion issue either directly or indirectly.

7

CHRISTIAN FAITH AND ABORTION

In this lesson:

▶ General statement of the issues involved
▶ Scriptures that mention the unborn
▶ Objections to this use of Scripture
▶ Treatment of abortion in church history

"How is a married woman able to plan schooling or commit herself
to a career or vocation as long as her life is continually open
to the disruption of unplanned pregnancies? Unless, of course,
she can fall back on an abortion when all else has failed!"
—Virginia Ramey Mollenkott, Christian feminist

"Recall the young Mary was pregnant under circumstances that *today routinely terminate in abortion. In the important theological context of Christmas, the killing of the unborn child is a symbolic killing of the Christchild."*

—Paul Vitz, New York University psychologist

Both Scripture and Christian tradition take an approach to human relationships, especially the relationship between parent and child, that differs radically from approaches taken by many in our "rights-oriented" culture.

The "rights" talk of abortion advocates wrongly construes the relationship between unborn child and mother in adversarial terms instead of the love towards which Christians are called.

From a distinctively Christian point of view, the "rights" talk employed by many advocates of abortion wrongly construes the relationship between unborn child and mother in adversarial terms, fetal rights vs. mother's rights, when the relationship should be instead one of love. Neither the child nor the mother is seen as an individual competing to achieve autonomously independent existence, but as a member of the Christian community, which is itself called to express love by protecting both child, a gift from God, and mother.

The Christian ethic from earliest times opposed abortion as a part of its special concern for widows, orphans, the poor, and the unborn (see *Didache* 2.2). Scripture proclaims God to be the author of life and witnesses to its high value even before birth. Together Scripture and Christian tradition value children and the ethic of love and self-sacrifice highly, and thus conflict fundamentally with the choice to abort.

THE BIBLE AND THE UNBORN

The Bible does not mention the word "abortion." It does, however, teach that murder — the unjustified killing of a human person — is wrong (Exod. 20:13). And it follows from this that if the Bible also teaches that the unborn are human persons, then it would be just as morally wrong to kill the unborn. So the real question is whether the Bible teaches that the unborn are human persons, not whether the Bible mentions or directly prohibits abortion. I believe that the following passages are sufficient to show that the Bible clearly teaches the full humanity of the unborn, although it is not an exhaustive list.[1]

> The real question is whether the Bible teaches that the unborn are human persons.

Personal Language Applied to the Unborn

There are a number of passages in the Bible which apply personal language to the unborn from conception. Genesis 4:1 reads: "Now the man had relations with his wife Eve, and she conceived and gave birth to Cain." Commenting on this passage, theologian John Jefferson Davis has observed that "the writer's interest in Cain extends back beyond his birth, to his conception. That is when his personal history begins. The individual conceived and the individual born are one and the same, namely, Cain." What follows from this is that Cain's "conception, birth, and postnatal life form a natural continuum, with the God of the covenant involved at every stage."[2]

In Job 3:3, the author writes: "Let the day perish on which I was to be born. And the night, *which* said, 'A boy [*geber*] is conceived.'" This passage connects the individual born with the individual conceived. "Job traces his personal history back beyond his birth to the night of conception. The process of conception is described by the biblical writer in personal terms. There is no abstract language of the 'product of conception,' but the concrete language of humanity."[3] It is interesting to note that the Hebrew word, *geber*, is translated as "boy" and specifically applied to the unborn, although it is usually used to describe *postnatal* humans and translated "male," "man," or "husband" (see Ps. 34:9; 52:9; 94:12; Prov. 6:34).[4]

Another passage, Psalm 51:5, states: "Behold, I was brought forth in iniquity, And in sin my mother conceived me." Again, we have evidence that one's beginning of existence can be traced back to conception.

The Unborn Are Called "Children."

The Bible refers to the unborn in the same way as it refers to infants and young children. In Luke 1:41,44 the word "baby" (*brephos*) is applied to the unborn: "And it came about that when Elizabeth heard Mary's greeting, the baby leaped in her womb; and Elizabeth was filled with the Holy Spirit. . . . 'For behold, when the sound of your greeting reached my ears, the baby leaped in my womb for joy.'" Compare this with Luke 2:12,16 where the infant Jesus is called a "baby" (*brephos*): "'And this *will be* a sign for you: you will find a baby wrapped in cloths, and lying in a manger.' . . . And they came in haste and found their way to Mary and Joseph, and the baby as He lay in the manger."

> In Luke 1:41,44 the word "baby" is applied to the unborn John.

The Unborn Are Known by God in a Personal Way.

A number of biblical passages clearly state that God knows the unborn in a personal way:

> For thou didst form my inward parts; Thou didst weave me in my mother's womb. I will give thanks to Thee, for I am fearfully and wonderfully made; Wonderful are Thy works, And my soul knows it very well. My frame was not hidden from Thee, When I was made in secret, *And* skillfully wrought in the depths of the earth. Thine eyes have seen my unformed substance; And in Thy book they were all written, The days that were ordained *for* me, When as yet there was not one of them (Ps. 139:13-16).

> Listen to Me, O islands, And pay attention, you peoples from afar. The Lord called Me from the womb; From the body of My mother He named Me (Isa. 49:1).

> Before I formed you in the womb I knew you, And before you were born I consecrated you; I have appointed you a prophet to the nations (Jer. 1:5).

> Then the angel of the Lord appeared to the woman, and said to her, "Behold now, you are barren and have borne no *children*, but you shall conceive and give birth to a son." . . . Then the woman came and told her husband, saying, "A man of God came to me and his appearance was like the appearance of the angel of God, very awesome. . . . But he said to me, 'Behold, you shall conceive and give birth to a son, and now you shall not drink wine or strong drink nor eat any unclean thing, for the boy shall be a Nazirite to God *from the womb to the day of his death.'*" (Judg. 13:3,6,7 — second italics my emphasis).

Objection to This Use of Scripture

Some authors, such as Robert Wennberg, have questioned the use of Scripture to establish the personhood of the unborn. Concerning those passages which use personal language to describe the unborn, Wennberg writes that "such references designate individuals not only before birth but before conception . . , and so they are not really to the point."[5] One problem with this criticism is that it is not applicable to all such passages, for some do speak exclusively of personal existence beginning at conception (e.g., Genesis 4:1 and Job 3:3). Another problem is that none of these passages claim that the persons in question existed prior to their conception, but rather, that God *knew* them or had plans for them before conception. This is certainly possible for an eternal God, who knows all things simultaneously (see Ps. 147:5; Job 28:24; Isa. 41:21-24; 46:10) and is not bound by time or space (see Ps. 90:2; Isa. 40:28; 43:12b,13; 57:15a), since he is the Creator of time and space (see Acts 17:25; Col. 1:16,17; Heb. 11:3; Rev. 4:11). That is, it is possible for him to know each and every one of us "before" we were conceived. Thus, such foreknowledge of human persons *prior to their conception* cannot be cited in order to explain away either conception as the beginning of personal existence or that personal existence is attributed to prenatal life when a passage in question *specifically* says, for example, that a certain individual either has personally existed from conception (e.g., Genesis 4:1) or has personally existed prior to birth (e.g., Jer. 1:5; Ps. 139:13-16; Luke 1:41-44). Moreover, the word "conception" or "to conceive" implies a genesis or a beginning, such as when I say, "This is the finest idea I have ever conceived." Hence, when God speaks of a person prior to conception, he is making a knowledge claim and not a claim about the person's existence. In light of these clarifications, the burden of proof is on Wennberg to show us why the more simple and clearly natural interpretation of the above passages should be abandoned.

Wennberg puts forth a second argument:

> Extending our examination, it would be a mistake to argue that since it was David who *was being formed* [or "brought forth" in NASB] in his mother's womb (Ps. 51:5) it must therefore have been David *the person* who was in his mother's womb. That would be to confuse "formation/creation" of a thing with the "completion/existence" of that thing. The fact is that an entity can be on the way to becoming a particular thing without it being that thing. It is quite natural for us to refer to what is in the process of becoming (the zygote or fetus in a Semite woman's womb) in terms of what it will eventually become (a King David), but we are not then speaking with technical accuracy. If a butterfly *is being formed* in a cocoon, it does not follow that there *is* a butterfly there (rather than a caterpillar or something betwixt or between).[6]

Wennberg seems to be arguing that one cannot cite passages such as Psalm 51:5 to show that the unborn are human persons, because such passages are only saying that the person in question is "being formed" not that the human being in the womb has become *that* person. There are several problems with this argument. First, even if Wennberg's interpretation of passages such as Psalm 51:5 is correct, he would still have to deal with other passages, such as some of the ones we have already cited, which clearly state that individual personal existence begins at conception (e.g., Genesis 4:1).

Second, Wennberg commits a fallacy of biblical interpretation which James Sire calls "world-view confusion."[7] This fallacy "occurs whenever a reader of Scripture fails to interpret the Bible within the intellectual and broadly cultural framework of the Bible itself and uses instead a foreign frame of reference."[8] Wennberg's distinction between person and human being is an invention of some contemporary philosophers who argue that a human being becomes a person at some stage in his or her development. But as we saw in Lesson 5, this view is seriously flawed. Because Wennberg has the burden to prove that the author of the Psalms was assuming that there is a difference between human being and human person, and because he provides no reason for us to believe he has satisfied this burden, it is reasonable to conclude that Wennberg is *reading back* into David's assertion a perspective foreign to the biblical worldview.

> Wennberg has the burden to prove that the author of the Psalms was assuming a difference between human being and human person.

Third, Psalm 51:5 *does say* that "in sin *my* mother conceived *me*" (emphasis mine). This indicates that David's personal existence can be traced back to conception, since it was at conception that he asserts *he* was conceived. And if this is the case, then it seems natural to interpret the first half of Psalm 51:5 ("I was brought forth" or "I was being formed") as describing the subsequent physical development of *David* in the womb, which continues after birth into infancy, childhood, adolescence, and adulthood. Although Wennberg is correct in saying that "if a butterfly *is being formed* in a cocoon, it does not follow that there *is* a butterfly there (rather than a caterpillar or something betwixt or between)," the insect which is becoming the butterfly *is* still the *same* insect which was once a caterpillar and will be a butterfly.

In the same way, the being at conception is the same person who will become the infant, the child, the adolescent, the adult, and maybe even a philosopher. Thus, passages such as Psalm 51:5 are describing a *person* who is in the process of becoming, *not* a thing that is in the process of becoming a person.

THE TEACHING OF CHURCH HISTORY

There is a long and rich tradition in Christian church history, extending back to the Early Church Fathers, against the practice of abortion. Since the Early Church Fathers were much closer to the writing of the New Testament than we are today, it is reasonable to say that there is a *presumption* in favor of both their interpretation of Scripture and their application of its ethical teachings.

In the early church document, the *Didache* (second century A.D.), the "Teaching of the Twelve Apostles" as it has been called, the author writes, "You shall not kill a child in the womb or murder a new-born infant. . . . You shall not *slay the child* by abortions." The second-century Christian apologist, Athenagoras states, "We say that those women who use drugs to bring on abortion commit murder and will have to give an account to God for abortion . . . ." Another early

> "You shall not *slay the child* by abortions."

Church Father of the second century, Clement of Alexandria, writes: "But women who resort to some sort of deadly abortion drug kill not only the embryos but, along with it, all human kindness."[9] This ethic is echoed by other Christian writers of the same historical period:

Minucius Felix: In fact, it is among you that I see newly-born sons at times exposed to wild beasts and birds, or dispatched by the violent death of strangulation; and there are women who, by use of medical potions, destroy the nascent life in their wombs, and murder the child before they bring it forth . . . .

Tertullian: But with us murder is forbidden once and for all. We are not permitted to destroy even the foetus in the womb, as long as blood is still being drawn to form a human being. To prevent the birth of a child is to anticipate murder. It makes no difference whether one destroys a life already born or interferes with it coming to birth. One who will be a man is already one . . . .[10]

> "One who will be a
> man is already one."

Among the many thinkers in church history who have written against abortion are Basil the Great, John Chrysostom, Ambrose, Jerome, and Augustine. Although some, such as Thomas Aquinas, under the influence of Aristotle's erroneous biology, disputed as to when the unborn entity receives its soul (Thomas claimed it was at forty days for a male and eighty days for a female),[11] they nevertheless opposed abortion at any stage during prenatal development (though disputing if it was less serious prior to ensoulment), except when abortion is needed to save the life of the mother. Concerning the church's historical view of abortion, one study concludes:

> For the whole of Christian history until appreciably after 1900, so far as we can trace it, there was virtual unanimity amongst Christians, evangelical, catholic, orthodox, that, unless at the direct command of God, it was in all cases wrong directly to take innocent human life. Abortion and infanticide were grouped together as early as the writing called the *Didache* which comes from the first century after the crucifixion. These deeds were grouped with murder in that those

committing or co-operating in them were, when penitent, still excluded from Communion for ten years by early Councils. . . . The absolute war was against the deliberate taking of *innocent* life, not in the sense of sinless life, but in the sense of life which was *innocens* (not harming) . . . . We may note that this strictness constituted one of the most dramatic identifiable differences between Christian morality and pagan, Greek or Roman, morality.[12]

CONCLUSION

From a Christian perspective, there is no right to abortion, for both Scripture and church tradition teach that the unborn are human persons and that the relationship between mother and child ought to be one of love rather than the exercising of rights. In addition, the arguments used to deny that the Bible teaches a sanctity-of-life ethic fail.

> From a Christian perspective, there is no right to abortion.

It should be kept in mind, however, that one need not believe the Bible in order to be pro-life. For, as we have seen in Lessons 1 through 6, there are outstanding and persuasive nontheological arguments that one can marshal in defense of the sanctity-of-human-life ethic.

NOTES

1. For greater detail and defense of the biblical case against abortion rights, see Francis J. Beckwith, *Politically Correct Death: Answering the Arguments for Abortion Rights* (Grand Rapids: Baker, 1993), chapter 8; John

Jefferson Davis, *Abortion and the Christian* (Phillipsburg, NJ: Presbyterian & Reformed, 1984), pp. 35-62; and Norman L. Geisler, *Christian Ethics: Options and Issues* (Grand Rapids: Baker, 1989), pp. 142-146, 148.

2. Davis, *Abortion and the Christian*, p. 40.

3. Ibid., p. 41.

4. Ibid.

5. Robert Wennberg, *Life in the Balance: Exploring the Abortion Controversy* (Grand Rapids: Eerdmans, 1985), p. 62.

6. Ibid., p. 63.

7. James Sire, *Scripture Twisting* (Downers Grove, IL: InterVarsity, 1980), pp. 23-30, 127-144.

8. Ibid., p. 26.

9. As quoted in Nigel M. de S. Cameron and Pamela F. Sims, *Abortion: The Crisis in Morals and Medicine* (Leicester, England: Inter-Varsity, 1986), pp. 14, 28. The early church material Cameron and Sims cite is acquired from citations compiled in David Braine, *Medical Ethics and Human Life* (Aberdeen, 1982). For more on the early church's view on abortion, see Michael Gorman, *Abortion and the Early Church* (Downers Grove, IL: InterVarsity, 1982).

10. Cited in Cameron and Sims, *Abortion*, pp. 29-30.

11. See John T. Noonan, Jr., "Aquinas on Abortion," in *St. Thomas Aquinas on Politics and Ethics*, trans. and ed. Paul E. Sigmund (New York: Norton, 1988), pp. 245-248.

12. Braine, *Medical Ethics*, as cited in Cameron and Sims, *Abortion*, p. 29.

Reflecting on Lesson Seven

1. Why does the Christian tradition deny that the appeal to rights is an appropriate way to look at pregnancy, childbirth, and parenthood?

2. The Bible does not mention the word "abortion." Why is this fact not enough to show that the Bible does not teach a sanctity-of-human-life ethic?

3. In the Bible, personal language is applied to the unborn, the unborn are called "children," and the unborn are said to be known by God in a personal way. What are the biblical passages that establish these truths? How would one argue from these truths that the Bible teaches a sanctity-of-human-life ethic?

4. What are Wennberg's two arguments against the use of the Bible in establishing the unborn's personhood?

5. How and why do Wennberg's arguments fail to prove his point? What is "worldview confusion" and how does Wennberg's case fall prey to it?

6. What does Christian Church history have to say about abortion?

Consider this:

Review the arguments on both sides of the abortion issue. Where do you now stand? Have you changed your position since starting this study?

Appendix:

MISSING THE POINT
OF THE PRO-LIFE POSITION

THE CASE OF THE REPUBLICAN PARTY PLATFORM AND THE
HUMAN LIFE AMENDMENT PLANK

In the first lesson of this small book we saw that the most important question in the abortion debate is "Are the unborn human persons?" To employ an illustration used by Gregory P. Koukl:

> Imagine that your child walks up when your back is turned and asks, "Daddy, can I kill this?" What is the first thing you must find out before you can answer him? You can never answer the question "Can I kill this?" unless you've answered a prior question: What is it? That is the key question.[1]

Although this may seem simple to you, it does not seem to have penetrated the minds of most political and social commentators who discuss abortion as it relates to national and party politics in the United

States. A case in point: the Republican party and its intramural spat over its pro-life platform plank.

It is indeed unfortunate that the only major political party in the United States that has taken a stance for life is the Republican Party. (Of course, many Democrats are strongly pro-life even though their party has embraced a proabortion position in its national party platform.). There are, however, Republican party members, candidates, and elected officials who want to change their party's official stance. This is why during every presidential election year since 1980 the issue of abortion and the question of whether the pro-life plank should remain in the Republican party platform becomes a hot issue. And most media accounts of this debate claim that the plank is calling for a constitutional amendment to ban abortion *even though there is nothing in either the 1992 or 1996 platforms which calls for such an amendment.*

What is typically and incorrectly referred to as the "abortion plank" is the section of the platform which calls for a constitutional amendment to protect all human life regardless of venue or level of maturity. The 1992 plank reads: "We believe the unborn child has a fundamental right to life which cannot be infringed. We therefore affirm our support for a human life amendment to the Constitution, and we endorse legislation that the Fourteenth Amendment's protections apply to unborn children." The 1996 plank provides a slightly different reading.

The text in which both years' planks reside deals with issues of race relations, bigotry, the civil rights of women, and the rights of the handicapped, as well as the rights of the unborn. This portion of the 1992 platform, which is under the general heading of "Individual Rights," begins with these sentences: "The protection of individual rights is the foundation of opportunity and security. The Republican Party is unique in this regard. Since its inception, it has respected every person, even when that proposition was universally unpopular. Today, as in the day of Lincoln, we insist that no American's rights are negotiable."

Thus, the plank calls for extending our nation's moral progress toward the elimination of unjust discrimination to those who are the most vulnerable in the human family, the unborn. Consequently, when commentators and candidates refer to this section of the platform as primarily referring to abortion, they simply are not speaking accurately, and they are clearly not addressing their opinions to the essential claim put forth by the planks' authors: the unborn are members of the human community and deserve to be protected from unjust harm.

The only time abortion is opposed in the 1992 platform is in terms of government funding, which is hardly a call for a constitutional amendment to ban abortion. Although abortion is mentioned more explicitly in the 1996 platform, an antiabortion constitutional amendment is nowhere to be found. Like its 1992 version, the 1996 platform both calls for the ending of public funding for organizations that advocate abortion as well as commends and supports those who provide abortion alternatives such as adoption. The 1996 platform, however, discusses the latter in greater detail and makes the point that the party's call for protecting the unborn will not translate into punishment for women seeking abortions if this protection were to become part of the Constitution. The platform does call for the punishment of physicians and others who abridge the right to life of the unborn by performing procedures whose sole purpose is the destruction of prenatal human beings. In addition, the plank is critical of President Clinton's vetoing of the partial-birth abortion ban as well as his initial resistance to certain adoption measures put forth by the Republican-majority Congress.

Certainly it would be correct to conclude that if a human life amendment were to become part of our Constitution, statutes and court decisions (such as *Roe v. Wade*), which permit virtually unrestricted abortion, probably would be declared unconstitutional. But this is merely an inference from the passage of such an amendment.

It is clear, then, that the platform never mentions a direct ban on abortion because its authors no doubt understood, and its opponents are reticent to admit, that what is doing the moral work in the question of abortion is the status of the unborn. The authors took seriously Justice Blackmun's comments in *Roe v. Wade*: "The appellee and certain amici argue that the fetus is a 'person' within the language and meaning of the Fourteenth Amendment. In support of this, they outline at length and in detail the well-known facts of fetal development. If this suggestion of personhood is established, the appellant's case, of course, collapses, for the fetus' right to life would then be guaranteed specifically by the Amendment."[2]

Thus, when all is said and done, the debate over the human life amendment plank is not really about banning abortion. After all, imagine if the plank had said this: The Republican Party affirms a woman's right to terminate her pregnancy if and only if it does not result in the death of her unborn child. Disagreement over such a plank would not be over the morality of abortion per se; it would be over the question of whether the unborn are fully human.

In sum, most politically active Republicans, both pro-life and pro-choice, along with most members of the media and most Republican candidates, seem not to have read the national platform. This is why it is not surprising that most of them do not seem to understand what the platform debate is supposed to be about. It is supposed to be about the plank, a plank which calls for our Constitution clearly and unequivocally in its text to assert that the human community includes both born and unborn from the moment of conception until natural death, and for that reason, unborn persons, like their postnatal brethren, should be protected from unjust harm.

NOTES

1. Gregory P. Koukl, *Precious Unborn Human Persons* (San Pedro, CA: Stand to Reason, 1999), p. 4.

2. *Roe v. Wade* 410 U.S. 113, 157-58 (1973).

FOR FURTHER STUDY

Books and Articles

Beckwith, F.J. *Politically Correct Death: Answering the Arguments for Abortion Rights.* Grand Rapids: Baker, 1993.

_____. "Disagreement without Debate: The Republican Party and the Human Life Amendment Plank." *Nexus: A Journal of Opinion* (Chapman Univ. School of Law) 4.1 (Spring 1999).

Boonin-Vail, D. "A Defense of 'A Defense of Abortion': On the Responsibility Objection to Thomson's Argument." *Ethics* 107.2 (January 1997).

Brody, B. *Abortion and the Sanctity of Human Life: A Philosophical View.* Cambridge, MA: M.I.T. Press, 1975.

Brown, H.O.J. *Death before Birth.* Nashville: Thomas Nelson, 1975.

Cameron, N. de S. M., and P.F. Sims. *Abortion: The Crisis in Morals and Medicine.* Leicester, England: Inter-Varsity, 1986.

Dworkin, R. *Life's Dominion: An Argument about Abortion, Euthanasia, and Individual Freedom.* New York: Knopf, 1993.

Ginsburg, R.B. "Some Thoughts on Autonomy and Equality in Relation to *Roe v. Wade*," *University of North Carolina Law Review* (1985).

Kamm, F.M. *Creation and Abortion: A Study in Moral and Legal Philosophy.* New York: Oxford University Press, 1992.

Koop, C.E., and F.A. Schaeffer. *Whatever Happened to the Human Race?* Old Tappan, NJ: Revel, 1979.

Koukl, Gregory. *Precious Unborn Human Persons.* San Pedro, CA: Stand to Reason, 1999.

Lee, P. *Abortion and Unborn Human Life.* Washington, DC: The Catholic University of America Press, 1996.

Marquis, D. "Abortion." *The Encyclopedia of Philosophy Supplement.* Donald M. Borchert, ed. New York: Simon & Schuster Macmillan, 1996.

_____. "Why Abortion Is Immoral." *The Journal of Philosophy* 86 (1989).

McInerny, P. "Does a Fetus Already Have a Future-Like-Ours?" *The Journal of Philosophy* 87 (1990).

Moreland, J.P., and S.B. Rae. *Body and Soul.* Downers Grove, IL: InterVarsity, 2000.

Norcross, A. "Killing, Abortion, and Contraception: A Reply to Marquis." *The Journal of Philosophy* 87 (1990).

Olasky, M. *Abortion Rites: A Social History of Abortion in America.* Wheaton, IL: Crossway, 1992.

Pavlischek, K. "Abortion Logic and Paternal Responsibilties: One More Look at Judith Thomson's 'A Defense of Abortion.'" *Public Affairs Quarterly* 7 (October 1993).

Pojman, L.P., and F.J. Beckwith, eds. *The Abortion Debate 25 Years after Roe v. Wade: A Reader.* 2nd edition. Belmont, CA: Wadsworth, 1998.

Schwarz, S.D. *The Moral Question of Abortion.* Chicago: Loyola University Press, 1990.

Sider, R. *Completely Pro-Life: Building a Consistent Stance.* Downers Grove, IL: InterVarsity, 1997.

Steinbeck, B. *Life before Birth: The Moral and Legal Status of Embryos and Fetuses.* New York: Oxford University Press, 1992.

Sumner, L.W. *Abortion and Moral Theory.* Princeton, NJ: Princeton University Press, 1981.

Thomson, J.J. "A Defense of Abortion." *Philosophy and Public Affairs.* 1 (1971).

Tooley, M. *Abortion and Infanticide.* New York: Oxford University Press, 1983.

Tribe, L. *Abortion: The Clash of Absolutes.* New York: W.W. Norton, 1990.

Wardle, L., and M.A.Q. Wood. *A Lawyer Looks at Abortion.* Provo, UT: Brigham Young University Press, 1982.

Warren, M.A. "On the Moral and Legal Status of Abortion." *The Monist* 57 (1973).

Wennberg, R. *Life in the Balance: Exploring the Abortion Controversy.* Grand Rapids: Eerdmans, 1985.

Wolf-Devine, C. "Abortion and the 'Feminine Voice.'" *Public Affairs Quarterly* 3 (July 1989).

Online Prolife Resources

American Bioethics Advisory Commission. (www.all.org/abac)

Americans United for Life. (www.unitedforlife.org)

Canadian Physicians for Life. (www.physiciansforlife.ca)

Center for Bioethics and Human Dignity. (www.bioethix.org)

Family Reseach Council. (www.frc.org)

National Right to Life. (www.nrlc.org)

Stand to Reason. (www.str.org) Offers the most outstanding lay training in defending the Christian worldview and the prolife position in particular.

Ultimate Prolife Resource List. (www.prolifeinfo.org)
University Faculty for Life. (www.mu.edu/ufl)

Prolife Graduate Programs in Bioethics

Trinity International University. (www.tiu.edu) T.I.U. offers an M.A. in bioethics at its graduate school in both Deerfield, Illinois (www.tiu.edu) and southern California (www.tls.edu). The southern California campus, Trinity Law School, also offers a dual degree program in which a student may earn both a law degree (J.D.) and the M.A. in bioethics. Seminary students at T.I.U.'s Trinity Evangelical Divinity School (in Illinois) may major in bioethics.

Talbot School of Theology, Biola University (www.biola.edu) Talbot, located in southern California, offers an M.A. in philosophy of religion and ethics with a strong bioethics component for students who want to concentrate in that area.

ABOUT THE AUTHOR

Francis J. Beckwith (PhD, Fordham) is associate professor of philosophy, culture, and law, and W. Howard Hoffman scholar, Trinity Graduate School, Trinity International University, where he also holds adjunct appointments in both Trinity Law School and Trinity Evangelical Divinity School. He is Senior Research Fellow, Nevada Policy Research Institute and Fellow at the Center for Bioethics and Human Dignity, the Bannockburn Institute.

His books include *Relativism: Feet Firmly Planted in Mid-Air* (Baker), *Politically Correct Death: Answering the Arguments for Abortion Rights* (Baker), *See the gods Fall: Four Rivals to Christianity* (College Press), *The Abortion Controversy 25 Years after Roe v. Wade: A Reader*, 2nd ed. (Wadsworth), *Do the Right Thing* (Wadsworth), *Affirmative Action: Social Justice or Reverse Discrimination?* (Prometheus), and *Are You Politically Correct?: Debating America's Cultural Standards* (Prometheus). He is also co-editor of the Critical Issues in Bioethics monograph series published by Eerdmans.

A member of the executive committees of both the Society of Christian Philosophers and the Evangelical Philosophical Society, as well as the board of directors of University Faculty for Life, Professor Beckwith's articles and reviews have been published in numerous journals such as *Social Theory and Practice; Journal of Social Philosophy; Public Affairs Quarterly; International Philosophical Quarterly; Nexus: A Journal of Opinion* (Chapman School of Law); *Journal of Law, Medicine and Ethics; Trinity Law Review; Ethics & Medicine; Faith and Philosophy; Canadian Philosophical Review; Focus on Law Studies; Philosophia Christi;* and *Journal of the Evangelical Theological Society.*